THE SOLO FEMALE TRAVEL BOOK

TIPS AND INSPIRATION FOR WOMEN WHO WANT TO SEE THE WORLD ON THEIR OWN TERMS

Jen Ruiz

The Solo Female Travel Book
Tips and Inspiration for Women Who Want to See the
World on Their Own Terms

Published by Jen on a Jet Plane
www.jenonajetplane.com

© 2019 Jen on a Jet Plane

Cover: Michelle Fontaine

Table of Contents

Introduction

Wanderlust: (n.) a strong desire for or impulse to wander
or travel and explore the world

I was 17 when I realized I could navigate Europe independently using just my "Europe for Dummies" guide. My mom booked a 10-day tour as a high school graduation gift and we hit all the big-name highlights: Rome, Venice, Paris and London with the added bonus of Lucerne, Switzerland along the way.

It was wonderful being abroad and making those memories together, but parts of the organized tour, which she bought through a AAA agent after months of comparing packages, were lackluster. We were being herded through exhibits with 50 or so people all following a random flag. At one point we ate frozen ham and peas for dinner while in Italy (a trauma from which I'll never fully recover). We spent days of our trip being transported between cities on a bus, crammed in square-foot spaces for eight hours at a time.

We could do better, so I took advantage of our designated "free time" to plan our own adventures. With the help of my book, we took a speedboat out to the islands of Venice, where we bought a Burano glass statue that my mom still has to this day. We rode the train to Stonehenge and were convinced that aliens really do exist. We saw a Shakespeare play at the Globe Theatre in London.

It didn't escape me that in addition to having a more personalized experience, we were saving money. By planning our experiences directly, we paid less than if we'd gone on the tour add-ons, and we got to do things our way.

I was hooked. Never has a person felt prouder holding a book that called them a dummy. I worshipped the guide because it held all I needed to know in one place, from train routes to activity suggestions. It was like the almanac from Back to the Future, making sure our trip went off without a hitch.

When I started traveling alone as a young professional some years later, planning was my safety blanket. The first few trips I took abroad by myself, I planned out my itinerary out to the *minute*. I read every attraction review and made full use of Google's street view option to see satellite pictures of where I'd be staying. I printed out all my tickets and advanced reservations. In retrospect this was wasteful, but something about having a folder full of confirmed purchases soothed my travel anxiety.

Today, I travel confidently knowing that I have the tools to tackle any challenge that awaits me, abroad or at home. If I forget something or lose something while traveling, I can get a replacement. If I become sick or miss a reservation, there's always a solution and way to move forward. That's what traveling alone has taught me. Like countless others before me, I've found the power of flying solo. Now, I want to help you do the same.

By way of introduction, my name is Jen Ruiz and I'm the lawyer turned solo female travel blogger behind Jen on a Jet Plane. My journey started when I set out to take 12 trips in 12 months while employed full-time as an attorney before my 30th birthday. I ended up taking 20 trips in 12 months, finding deals like a $70 roundtrip flight to Aruba, $22 roundtrip flight to San Francisco and $16 flight to Ecuador. People asked me how I did it, so I wrote a book called "The Affordable Flight Guide: How to Find Cheap Airline Tickets and See the World on a Budget." It became a #1 Amazon bestseller and 2018 Readers' Favorite Award winner.

That's when I did something really scary: I quit my job practicing law to travel and write instead. I sold all of my belongings (except for my dresses, travel memorabilia and limited-edition Beauty and the Beast DVD) and started living as a digital nomad.

Solo travel has brought me experiences I could have never imagined. I know what it's like to climb Huayna Picchu in Peru, enter a volcano in Iceland and see a cave lit by glowworms in New Zealand.

That's why I wrote this book – to share inspiration, funny fails and practical tips for anything thinking about going on a solo trip. I want you to be your "Solo Travel for Dummies," and hope to earn every bit of respect that title deserves.

At the end of this guide, I've included two free resources. The first is a list of 10 apps, groups and websites to help you meet people abroad since loneliness is a common deterrent amongst would-be solo travelers. The second is a list of 12 things you should do the night before your trip to allow you to travel with peace of mind.

You can also visit my website, Jen on a Jet Plane, to find articles on remote work, budget travel and destinations around the world.

Are you ready to start seeing the world on your own? Let's get started!

SOLO TRAVEL TIP #1
Never Get Caught in the Grand Canyon After Dark

I was having one of those nights where I couldn't fall asleep and was mindlessly scrolling through Facebook and Instagram, clicking links in bios and watching every cute animal interaction posted in the last 24 hours. Facebook just sends these videos my way now without friends sharing the clip or me even following the page. They say it's "because they think I'll like it." What can I say? They're not wrong.

This particular flare-up of my chronic screen addiction, a disease affecting anyone with a smartphone after 2007, came on a random Wednesday in April. My eyes were half open, my thumb sore from swiping. Sometimes I worry about arthritis in the future; it doesn't look good.

I had to be up early for work and intended to do the responsible thing and go to sleep early, but more than 3 hours had passed since I got into bed. I was scrolling through a calendar of dates on a third-party website.

January — nothing.

February — nothing.

I went all the way to November and was ready to call it a night when it happened. Suddenly, a date popped up. My left eye, having already closed, sprung open. I came to life, sitting straight up and staring at the screen, the text blurring as my eyes adjusted to the light. I brought the cell phone within inches of my face, just to be sure.

One night only. One night out of the entire year that was available. The adrenaline kicked in, jolting me from my pre-sleep stupor with a find of this magnitude. I tried to take it in quickly since there was a five-minute countdown clock running in the bottom left corner, threatening to release my ticket.

My thumb had somehow navigated me to an available camping permit for Havasu Falls, Arizona. This wasn't just any permit – Havasu Falls is one of the toughest hiking permits to get, right up there with The Wave, and requires planning well in advance. Tickets sell out the same day they go on sale in February for the rest of the *year*. In April, there was no chance of finding a permit – you were two months too late.

Those who do score a permit are treated to views of pristine waterfalls on the Havasupai reservation in the heart of the Grand Canyon. It's a 20-mile return hike to get to the first waterfall and the grounds can't otherwise be accessed without a permit or reservation at the Havasupai Lodge.

The timer was down to three minutes and I was seriously considering it. I opened up another window in private browsing mode to see if there were any other permits available – one night is nice but two would be even better. As I suspected, no luck. All the calendar months were empty. Two minutes left.

I thought about the price -- $140 seemed like a lot of money to spend on a whim, especially to sleep outside. As a rule, I try to avoid making credit card purchases at 1 a.m., and that price didn't take into account any taxes or fees. I'd have to charge it, and permits were nonrefundable. Not to mention I'd still have to figure out a plane ticket.

Down to one minute. It was now or never. I thought about the next time I would get this opportunity. At the earliest, it would be another year. At worse, never. I wasn't looking for it, but the universe was calling me to the Grand Canyon.

As the countdown clock entered the last 10 seconds, I clicked "book now," submitting my details and securing a one-night camping permit to visit Havasu Falls in November, seven months down the road. I tried not to dwell about the impromptu expense and went to sleep thinking of turquoise blue waterfalls.

Months passed and I wanted to train, I really did, but life happened. I did workout videos online for a few weeks before I went, 20-30 minutes a day. Unfortunately, that wasn't quite the same as the physical challenge that awaited me.

My stepdad helped me pack. He's an avid camper and had most of the supplies I needed. It's a good thing, too. Did you know camping gear is expensive? From tents to sleeping bags, "roughing it" can add up.

I almost chickened out. I had a friend who made the trip in October and came back missing eight out of ten toenails. It may sound vain or shallow to seasoned hikers, but I am very attached to my toenails. All ten of them. Unlike my friend, I didn't have a guide, so I feared I'd end up worse.

I flew into Las Vegas the night before my hike and rented a car to make the drive out to my hotel, about an hour from the trailhead. I was in the drive-through of an In-N-Out Burger when the worker asked me if I wanted to a "double-double." I said "yes, yes," and parked to devour my meal in the middle of the Arizona desert, contemplating if I should turn back. It was approaching midnight, only a few hours before my hike. I took comfort in knowing that if In-N-Out Burger was my last meal, I'd chosen wisely.

I was up at 4 a.m. and scheduled to hit the trail by 7 a.m. As I drove further into the desert, my phone lost service. I went from listening to Pandora to scanning through radio stations in hopes of stumbling onto something that resembled music. I was driving the rental car I'd picked up the night before, so it didn't occur to me to fill up the gas tank in the morning. As I drove, the area became less populated, and my tank increasingly empty.

That's when a wild pig crossed my path. It was a dark, spotted hog that jutted across the small highway, adding some variation to the otherwise repetitive scene. I saw the pig with enough time to avoid it, though I will say for a pig it moved remarkably fast. I looked at the fuel gauge and saw it was approaching the halfway mark. I didn't realize I'd driven that much but figured there had to be a gas station up ahead.

Shortly after that the electricity lines stopped. There were no stores, no people, no signs of civilization. Just a desert highway hopefully heading in the right direction.

That's when a moose crossed my path. It was a big moose – the first one I've ever seen in real life but with definite Bullwinkle properties. One animal was a sighting, two was starting to seem like a sign.

My tank was below the halfway mark. More than a half hour had passed and I was trying to calculate the miles per gallon used by the car, the number of miles I had left and whether I had enough gas for a return trip. It was a convoluted word problem that kept ending in me stranded by the side of the road without cell service or transportation. I started to freak out.

That's when a third, unidentified animal crossed my path. I couldn't make sense of what it was, and at this point I didn't need any more convincing. I decided to turn around and refuel at the last gas station I'd seen before entering the 60-mile stretch and final road to the trailhead.

I got back to the gas station around 7:30 a.m. with less than a quarter tank of gas left. The attendant told me I'd made the right decision coming back – there was nothing at the trailhead except for a parking lot.

It's always fun to find this information out through trial and error. At least I'd erred on the side of caution and secured my ride back. I hit the road once again to the Hualapai Hilltop, this time with no animals crossing my path. I had the "all clear" from the universe.

Perhaps it was because I'd worked myself up over it so much, or because I was frustrated that I didn't think of something as basic as gas, but I felt a renewed resolve to tackle this hike. I'd come this far and I was going to see it through.

I took the first parking spot available when I arrived. This turned out to be a little too eager since I later realized I parked near the wrong entrance, but I kept walking anyway. I knew every step coming out of the hike would be painful and I'd resent myself for parking further unnecessarily but I was already late and that was tomorrow's problem -- literally.

I hit the trail at 9 a.m., feeling like I was last person to get started that day. Before my empty tank scare, I was naïve and thought I could make it to all three waterfalls in one day. However, it's eight miles into the canyon just to reach the reservation. From there it's another 2 miles to the campsite and Havasu Falls, then a half mile further to Mooney Falls and Beaver Falls is still 3 miles beyond that. I adjusted my goal to something more realistic – see a waterfall, come back alive, don't get caught in the Grand Canyon after dark.

It turns out backpacks get heavy when you're hiking with them for hours on end. I made sure everything in mine was essential, down to the can of Beefaroni, but it weighed on me. I tightened the straps around my hips and chest and ignored the pain starting to shoot down my neck and back.

I invested in nice hiking boots and have never been more pleased with a purchase. In the store, they felt like walking on air. That feeling didn't last long into the hike as I started to get blisters but at no point did I feel like my toenails were in peril (thank goodness!).

The sun in the canyon was unrelenting. Hikers are exposed to the elements on most of the walk and it's almost like a labyrinth. There are no signs or people telling you which way to go, just dozens of diverging dirt paths all presumably heading in the same direction down the canyon.

I made it to the Havasupai Reservation at 2 p.m. after five hours of hiking. The sight of houses and stores after seeing nothing but rock formations after an hour felt like walking into an oasis. I stopped by a fence and marveled at the village that the tribe built in this vast clearing. For an American destination, this was about as remote as you could get.

I spotted a sign for fry bread and walked towards the building. It was a small store so you had to leave your backpack outside, probably for fear of people clumsily knocking down items on the shelf. This was a wise precaution since my coordination was not at its peak at that moment. I saw coconut water in the fridge and practically floated to it. After drinking water from a pouch warmed by my back all day, boxed coconut water felt gourmet.

I asked for fry bread but was told I was in the wrong store and would need to walk further into town for my meal. Challenge accepted. I grabbed my coconut water and put my chains – erm, backpack – back on to walk towards lunch.

I marched resolutely into the town center. I craved the deep-fried goodness of carbs and had worked up an appetite. When I made it to the café and was relieved to find they took credit cards, meaning I could *really* feast. I ordered a large pineapple juice, fry bread, hamburger and fries. I ate it all in less than 5 minutes. I'm not even sure I chewed it.

As much as I wanted to take a nap after that, I was still 2 miles away from the camp. I grabbed my bag again and walked on, this time full from lunch.

When I heard the sounds of a waterfall, I was reanimated. I started running like a contestant who just got picked to be on The Price is Right. I was intent on finding the iconic viewpoint I'd seen in so many Instagram photos and thought this would be the moment to reward all my efforts.

I was wrong. This was a smaller waterfall known as Lower Navajo Falls. It's so small no one really talks about it. In any other place it'd be the main attraction, but the waterfalls of the Havasupai territory are so stunning that this seemed less than impressive in comparison. It's like finding fool's gold at the end of a rainbow. Deflated, I kept going. Not before taking plenty of pictures though, in case I collapsed and this was the closest I got to a waterfall, period.

I walked for another hour before desperately asking the next couple I saw walking in the opposite direction, "excuse me, how much further??"

They looked at me sympathetically, reassuring me that they'd been exhausted after their hike and that I wasn't far from the campsite.

I walked about 50 feet further and then I saw it. The million-dollar view of Havasu falls, with its blue waters contrasting against the red-hued limestone, made even more vibrant by a riverbed of reflective rocks. It was a real-life dream. I sat, exhausted, and took it all in.

But first, I took 50 or so selfies with the waterfall. Horizontal, vertical, pointing at the falls, looking back at the falls. Then I asked a passerby to take a picture of me. I normally carry a tripod when I travel solo but it didn't make the essentials list when I was packing.

The campground was just a little further, down two dozen or so stairs. I crossed that campground entrance like a marathon runner crossing the finish line. I didn't go far — first empty spot I saw was as good a place as any to set up camp. I wasn't picky, I just wanted to lay down. That night, I cooked my Beefaroni outside my tent while still sitting in the tent. Then I put on every piece of clothing I brought with me and did my best to get some rest despite a drop in temperature, no sleeping mat and a desperate need for a pillow.

The first day was done and like the memes say, I didn't die. The second day was murder. Bloody murder.

I stepped gingerly when I woke up to avoid the blisters I'd popped the night before. Over the course of the day, I would develop new blisters in places where I shifted my weight. Every step felt like sheer torture. The weight of the bag on my shoulders ached like an ice pick being shoved into alternating sides of my body.

I wanted to skip the hike and take a helicopter out, calling it a day by noon, so I was ecstatic when one of the tribe members passing by on horseback told me that the helicopters were running that day. I'd read otherwise online but there's not a lot of information about this place, so you never know.

I walked towards the reservation holding on to hope that an air rescue might be in order. I showed up to the helicopter field with a semi-delirious look on my face. The locals sitting nearby just shook their heads. As I suspected, the helicopters only ran on Thursdays, Fridays, Sundays and Mondays. I was there on Tuesday and Wednesday. There was no relief for me, and the only way out of the canyon was to walk through it. I limped over to the cafeteria, looking to numb my feelings with fry bread before having to face the grueling 8-mile journey.

Hours later I found myself in the middle of the Grand Canyon yet again, this time going significantly slower. At one point it had been a while since I'd seen anyone else on the trail and I got worried. Several black birds started circling overhead, as if they could smell death.

When I reached the final half-mile stretch, I was so relieved. I was beginning to think I was the last person in the Canyon and seriously worried I wouldn't make it out by nightfall despite having begun the trek at 7am.

I wanted to run to the exit when I saw it. I wanted to sprint like Rocky to my car. But I physically couldn't. I sat down no less than a dozen times in the last tenth of a mile alone, taking a break every few steps. It was only when I heard a coyote that I finally forced myself over the threshold, right as the sun was setting.

In the end, I made it to Havasu Falls and back, solo, on my very first overnight backpacking trip. Even better, I kept all my toenails!

Don't ever let anyone tell you that you can't do something. Don't sit out from a challenge just because you're scared or alone. Even if you have to hobble your way through, just keep putting one foot in front of the other and I promise it is going to be the difference between living the life of your dreams and simply wondering "what if."

As for my next hike, let's give it a little bit of time. Thankfully, I have the memories of fry bread and waterfalls to hold me over till then.

1.1 Travel More, Worry Less

What if I'd never pressed "book" on that campground reservation?

What if I'd chickened out after my double-double?

What if I'd interpreted a moose, pig and unidentified animal crossing my path as a sign to go home?

There are so many choices we take, each with the ability to lead us down a different path. You can let fear grip you and wish you'd taken a chance later or you can leap and deal with the consequences as they come. The second option is scarier but if you try it, you might be surprised at what you're capable of. Take comfort in knowing that you're a savvy, intelligent, resourceful woman that can handle whatever is thrown at you.

I am always surprised when I hear friends say they have a fear of traveling solo. I'm talking about powerful women who have given birth multiple times, built businesses from the ground up and achieved the highest levels of education. Yet they're intimidated by something as trivial as dining alone. They walk in empty parking lots day after day in dangerous cities (Miami, New York, Los Angeles, Baltimore) yet they're afraid to walk elsewhere in the world.

Never be afraid to walk alone. Be afraid of standing still. Challenge yourself to meet new people, take in new surroundings and entertain new ideas. Traveling is just one of many ways to do this and I encourage you to do so every chance you get. You don't have to go far to have a worthwhile experience and it's an investment of time and money that you'll rarely regret, even when things go wrong.

If you're a Type A personality who thinks the words "go with the flow" are stress-inducing, don't worry. Traveling doesn't have to make you feel uneasy. You can be as detailed or rigid as you choose. That's the beauty of solo travel.

The only person you have to verify your schedule with is yourself. The only person whose interests you're catering to are your own. The tickets you have to buy or reservations you have to make are for one person.

Bonus: when you're traveling alone it's easier to snag upgrades or favors since you're only asking for one person.

Some would-be solo travelers might be hesitating for fear that friends or family wouldn't approve. When you are in a good place emotionally, friends and family will see that and understand why you travel. If they're worried, keep in touch while you're abroad with daily calls or emails. I still send my mom my itinerary, including flight and hotel information, before I go on a trip. Thank the people who love you for their concern but don't let your adult life be dictated by their fears or norms.

Traveling solo should not be a time for worrying – it should be a time for celebrating that you're lucky enough to have the freedom to travel and badass enough to know how to do it unaccompanied.

1.2 The Power of Flying Solo

Why am I so passionate about traveling solo? It's because I firmly believe in a thing called "solo travel magic." In a nutshell, solo travel magic occurs when you put yourself out there and the universe rewards you, sending people or messages your way to encourage you to continue on your path.

You may not see this at happening at first – it could be something as subtle as interacting with a shop owner who throws in a special bonus with your purchase, to a grand gesture like having a song dedicated to you at an opera. The latter is a true story and one of my most surreal moments, btw.

An example of solo travel magic could include someone offering to take a photo of you when you're struggling to take a selfie or giving you a coupon for a discount on a tour. I once had hotel staff give me a complimentary watercolor painting of the building to remember my stay. It was a lovely souvenir and one I wouldn't have been offered if the extent of my interaction with them had been handing over my credit card before heading to my room.

I hesitate to mention this because critics might attribute special treatment to being a young female. I've seen kindness shown to a 6-foot tall, 400-pound man. People take pride in their country and don't want tourists to leave with a bad impression. They will go out of their way to orient you, accommodate you and make you want to return, regardless of what you look like. All you have to do is be curious, respectful and make an effort to interact with your new surroundings in a meaningful way.

This sentiment is magnified when you're traveling alone. You have to be careful about the vibe you send out and the help you accept since you don't want to attract the wrong attention, but more often than not you'll find that acts of kindness are intended to brighten your day and help you make a nice memory, no strings attached.

If you're willing to put some time into making human connections, with staff or people you might not have thought to bond with, you'll be surprised at what you get in return. I recommend that you start looking at solo travel as a road to self-discovery. Stop fearing all the things that could go wrong and start looking forward to all the things that could go right.

You might find that, somewhere along the way, you start making your own magic.

1.3 Important Pre-Trip Considerations

1. *Do you need a visa for your destination? How much does it cost? How long can you stay? What's the renewal option?*

Travelers coming from the United States can visit 166 countries without a visa. Regulations vary depending on the country you're visiting. Perhaps you can only visit China visa-free for a less than a week as opposed to Europe, where you can stay for 90 days. You need to verify the specifics of the country you're visiting before buying your ticket. Entry to certain countries can require a visa application or payment of fees. Give yourself enough time to process all this before going, anywhere from a week to 30 days.

You don't need to register with your embassy unless you're going for an extended period of time or worried about your safety. You can check the State Department website for information on the current threat in that country but they'll tell you almost everywhere is dangerous. If you listen to them, you'll never go anywhere.

If you want to stay in a country for longer than just a vacation you can live and work with a work visa but you'll need proof of income and possibly sponsorship letters or an interview. Many countries allocate you a few months upon arrival to submit the appropriate paperwork to their offices.

2. *If you've bought a one-way ticket, will you need proof of a return ticket to be able to board?*

Sometimes you're so busy planning the bigger picture that you neglect the smaller aspects that have the potential to mess up your trip before it even begins. Airline agents are the gatekeepers to your vacation and you need to get past them first. Many times, if travel to your country of choice is restricted, they will require proof of ongoing travel in order to let you on the plane.

Some people have travel plans already made and are fine but those who don't get can around this by purchasing a ticket and then getting a refund. Thankfully, most airlines give you a 24-hour grace period by which to cancel even if your ticket is labeled "nonrefundable."

3. *Do you need vaccinations? Are there any medical concerns that you should consider before planning your trip? Are you seeking to have a procedure performed abroad? Will you have your period while traveling?*

You don't need to get vaccinated for every trip you take. Instead, consider them if you're going to a place with known health dangers. Consult your physician for more information.

Vaccines are something you want handled before your trip. We'll talk about finding a doctor abroad in the section about what to do in an emergency but stick to your own doctor and medicines as much as possible. It's confusing to decipher the active ingredients of medications while standing in a foreign pharmacy.

It could be possible that you're traveling to get a medical procedure done for less than it would cost in the U.S., a subsection of tourism that's growing fast. People choose to go abroad to avoid paying American health premiums on everything from face lifts to veneers. If this is the case, make sure you do your research ahead of time to find testimonies from the doctor's past patients.

Bring basic over the counter medications from home in your carry-on or checked luggage, including headache medicine like Tylenol or Aleeve (always bring more of this than you think you'll need), indigestion medicine, allergy medicine like Benadryl, band-aids of varied sizes, antibacterial ointment like Neosporin and a dry heat pack in case you pull a muscle or get cramps.

One area of concern for female travelers is going abroad during your period. If you're in Asia, for example, you'll have a hard time finding tampons. You can use a menstrual cup, but I still haven't gotten around to trying them so instead I take the individual tampons out of the box and stuff a pocket in my bag full of them, also throwing in some liners. I also find this is great place to store random things in my hotel room that I don't want found since people aren't likely to dig and feel around a pocket of tampons.

Another comment on this topic -- I was asked if I was on my period before entering a temple in Bali since being on your period makes you "impure" and you're prohibited from entering. I wondered who would verify my answer if I said I wasn't. Thankfully, they took me at my word so it was only as awkward as the initial inquiry.

If you're pregnant you'll need to consider how long you can stand being on an airplane and if the conditions of a new place will affect you physically, like extreme heat or dryness. Finally, if you get anxiety from busy cities or can't walk long distances, you'll want to take that into account in the early stages so you're not signing up for a destination that will ultimately be unenjoyable.

4. *Are there any must-see attractions, permits or reservations that require you to book well in advance? How far in advance? What's the best way to go about booking? Do you need to have a note on your calendar if sales open up on a specific day?*

There's no point in booking a trip to Machu Picchu if tickets are already sold out for your travel days. Similarly, it would be sad to miss out on a city's top attractions, like Da Vinci's painting of "The Last Supper in Milan" or the Alhambra in Granada, Spain because tickets were sold out before you got there and you didn't do your research and purchase ahead of time.

The first thing you need to do is make a master list of all the things you want to see in a new city. Since you're just browsing, any search tool will do. You can search for "top things to do in X city" on Google or enter "travel to X" in Pinterest to see what blog posts come up. You're looking for inspiration, itineraries and little-known gems.

Once you get your list of what you want to see and do, it's time to start doing your research. If you need tickets in advance, like with the campground permit for Havasu

Falls, make sure you mark the day that tickets go on sale in your calendar. If you're more than three months out, some European attractions or museums might not show availability yet. In that case, mark on your calendar to check for ticket availability the first of every month.

Another example is game shows and television screenings. You can be a member of the audience for a variety of different shows, from "Good Morning America" to "The Daily Show." Most of these shows are filmed in L.A. or New York so you'd have to be in the area but you can secure tickets for guest spots a month to three months in advance. You just have to be diligent about checking online. I did this and was able to attend a special screening of ABC's "The Chew" in Walt Disney World during the Food and Wine Festival. These experiences can add cherished memories to your vacation (fo' free!) but require some elbow work on your part.

Some people hate planning and prefer to leave it up to someone else to set the schedule. You can certainly do that, but 1) most tour providers charge more for solo travelers since you're not splitting the room charges and 2) you are capable of planning your own dream trip. Everyone's travel style is different so if your idea of indulgence is having someone else take care of all the planning and worrying for you, by all means, delegate on.

However, if you want to have unique experiences and call your own shots but are worried you don't have the skills, know-how or courage to do so, push that mentality aside. It is so much easier to navigate the world than you think, and a little advanced planning can go a long way. Knowledge is power, and you can learn anything on the internet nowadays.

5. *What is the primary language where you're going? Can you start learning and practicing key phrases before your trip?*

The best way to ingratiate yourself to the local people and show you're interested in interacting with your surroundings in a non-superficial way is to learn some of the local language. I don't expect you to be fluent – a few key phrases and words will do. Examples include "hello, nice to meet you" "thank you," "please," "good night," and "how much?"

I recommend you download DuoLingo, a free language learning app you can get on your cell phone. You can also find language audio tapes and software programs for free at your local library. Then, when you're traveling use the Google Translate app and pre-download the language files for your country so you can access Google translation even while offline. It's not always 100% accurate but it gets the job done in a pinch.

If you're staying somewhere long-term, I found a great way to make friends is by attending language events found through the Meetup website. People are there to talk, after all, and even if you don't speak another language you are an expert in English and would be the star of any English-learning attraction. I made friends this way when I went to a Spanish speakers' event in Australia.

1.4 Identifying Your Travel Style

There are different options for how you choose to travel. You can go with a guided tour that is pre-planned and have someone accompany you from start to finish. You can set your own schedule and book day-long excursions with a group. You can plan and do everything yourself. Finally, you can volunteer or work abroad. Let's talk about the pros and cons of them all.

GUIDED TOUR

I cringe when I hear "guided tour" as a solo traveler, because it usually means beaucoup bucks. If you have the money, however, it's worth paying for peace of mind. Tours have come a long way since my European disaster, with companies like G Adventures and Intrepid Travel offering experiences that are more immersive and fit the growing needs of the industry.

If you go this route, the tour company you choose will take care of the visas, hotels, food, advanced ticket reservations and transportation. You can sometimes pay through installments, spreading out your costs. The extent of your planning is entering your credit card information online, no stress, no deadlines, no worries.

If this sounds like you, by all means indulge. The only downside is these companies are efficient and run on a tight schedule, so you won't have time to linger if something catches your eye.

An alternative is to pay someone to organize a self-guided tour, where a company provides you with information handouts and background information and make all the reservations for your but doesn't send an in-person guide to accompany you. From what I've seen, these types of packages are several hundred dollars at a minimum.

Another option for those looking for a middle ground is to take a cruise. The ship has no shortage of activities on board, your destinations are pre-selected and food and accommodations are secured at the time of booking.

Traveling doesn't have to be a lot of work, and any of the three methods I've mentioned are a great way to see the world in a relaxed, carefree way.

GUIDED EXCURSIONS

Maybe you don't need a tour guide for the length of your trip, but it would be nice to have one for a particular destination. For instance, having a guide to help you navigate street markets in Asia is a great way to make sure you're eating reputable food and getting to try new dishes. Similarly, going on a walking tour of a particular neighborhood, like the Red Light District in Amsterdam, could add context and history to an otherwise awkward stroll.

In this case, you have a couple of options. There are websites that offer tours, like Viator and Get Your Guide. These prices will almost always be higher than anything you would secure by booking directly through the venue but come with pre-arranged transportation and vetted guides.

You can browse these tours and book the activities you like directly, like cooking classes at a certain venue or jewelry-making demonstrations at a famous store. You can also look for city passes that offer free admission or discounts to multiple places to see if they include the activities you'd like to do.

Sometimes if you're visiting a monument, you'll find last-minute guides offering tours on your way in. When I was at the Parthenon, I signed up for a tour with a woman recruiting people at the main entrance. Her price was reasonable and she already had tickets, meaning I could skip the line that spanned around the block. When you do this, you're taking a gamble on the guide since you can't pre-verify them through reviews or hold them accountable with a third-party company. Sometimes you get what you pay for, but some context is better than none. In my case with the Parthenon tour, it was brief, but the €15 price was worth getting to skip the line alone.

Another strategy is to look for free walking tours of a city. I've done these in Athens, San Francisco and Buenos Aires and was pleasantly surprised. They're run by volunteers who are seeking a tip at the end, so come prepared with cash. Generally, they're passionate about their work and eager to share relevant information with you.

SELF-GUIDED

If you're a do-it-yourselfer, it's probably because you like to save money and be in control. Personally, those are two of my favorite things. The good news is that you can plan your own way around most places. It's downright easy in cities that are accustomed to tourists, like Milan or Paris.

The self-guided route is best for people who have the time to plan accordingly beforehand and don't mind having to figure out and problem solve in the moment. If this is you, one of your essential items is a library card. Make sure to check out your library's travel section for free resources and maps. If your loan is long enough and you find a portable pocket guide, you can even bring it with you.

Another useful tool is the Rick Steves Europe app. While it's limited to one continent, it has informative and entertaining guides that you can use to do self-guided walking tours around Europe's biggest cities. I also recommend downloading the apps for any museums you enter, since they often offer free walking tours as well. Just make sure that whenever you're walking with headphones you have one off and one on to still be cognizant of your surroundings, especially if you're on the street.

The downside of being self-guided is that you can miss out on context. I went to see the cemetery where Eva Pedron is buried in Buenos Aires but was too early for the free guided tour. I was able to find the gravesite myself, but wish I'd had someone to explain to me the details about her final resting place, as well as the history behind this particular cemetery and other tidbits about the famous people buried there. Instead, I just saw a mausoleum with some flowers and felt a little disappointed.

History is fascinating, but without the proper explanation it can be dull. If you travel to see a site but have no idea what you're looking at, you're doing yourself a disservice and missing out on the best part of the experience – learning something new.

VOLUNTEER/WORK ABROAD

This last type of traveler is rarer than the three I've already covered. They like to give back and feel like they've made a difference instead of just lounging by a pool. If this sounds like you, there are experiences out there than can enrich your travels.

You can teach English to Buddhist monks at a monastery in Thailand. You can release baby sea turtles in the wild in Mexico. You can teach English abroad, long term or short term, everywhere from Oman to China. Sometimes you have to pay for these opportunities. Sometimes they're done on a work exchange basis where you get room and board in exchange for your time. Sometimes they're paid. I prefer the last option but you can find all three just by searching online. Websites like Workaway or Help Exchange are a great place to start.

Another option is housesitting. You may be interested in taking care of other people's houses and animals in exchange for a free place to stay. This can make traveling affordable, especially when you're staying somewhere for a month or more. A good way to start housesitting is by joining websites that connect you with potential clients, like Trusted Housesitters, Mind My House and Nomador. Build up your profile by taking on local gigs first and getting good reviews.

Finally, you can combine your day job with traveling. Companies like Remote Year send you around the world while you work remotely. The downside is that you have to pay them and they don't help you find remote work. You can ask to attend conferences abroad or bookend existing work trips with personal vacation days. You could also look for related work in your field, like doctors and nurses that volunteer abroad.

What's your travel style? Do you see yourself on cruise in the middle of the Mediterranean, seeing ports of call with expert guides that can fit in all the highlights on a short trip? Or do you see yourself cruising the Ring Road in Iceland, discovering places at your own pace at pulling over at unexpected sights? Would you rather rent an apartment, root down somewhere for a week and decide what you want to see in a city, like Hong Kong or Los Angeles? Do you like to work while traveling, knowing you're making a difference?

Be honest with yourself when you're answering these questions. Staying true to your travel style is key to having a good time, especially if you're traveling solo for the first time. You don't want to set yourself up on a massive hike unassisted through the Grand Canyon if you know you're the kind of person that feels comfortable with a guide and itinerary.

No matter your preferred manner of travel, there are unique experiences out there for you. Once you get a few successful solo trips under your belt, you'll be tempted to try them all.

SOLO TRAVEL TIP #2
Credit Card Rental Insurance Does Not Work in New Zealand

O n my last day in New Zealand I woke up ready for
some pancakes. I don't normally eat pancakes. I like
to eat eggs in the morning and fool myself into
thinking I'm going to be healthy for the rest of the day
because I got a good start.

Still, there I was, ready to stuff my face with the best
pancakes in Coromandel, New Zealand. I'd met a group of
locals at a trivia game I stumbled into while looking for
dinner the night before. Naturally, we became friends
(trivia is my element). I was invited to come for breakfast
at their restaurant this morning and couldn't say no.

It had been a stressful night – I barely made it back in one
piece. I was staying at a homestay/hotel in Coromandel,
which I chose for its proximity to the famous hot water
beach. It turns out, objects on Google maps are further
than they appear. What might have been a 20-minute drive
on flat streets turned into an hour-long drive on a curvy
mountain road with no barriers and cars going exceedingly
fast. I was still acclimating to driving on the other side of
the road – that 20-mile journey was petrifying, and I had
no idea what awaited me on the way back.

I made it just in time to catch the sunset and visit the hot water beach during low tide. It's a unique place that was worth the effort it took to get there. Guests bring their own shovels and dig holes in the sand to form natural hot tubs. The water and the sand are both warmed by the geothermal activity of the island, which rests on a series of volcanoes. I hopped from pool to pool, determined to find the warmest of them all and celebrate the small victory of having made it this far. It was the end of my New Zealand trip, and this was my last big stop.

I laid back in the sand and basked in the cotton candy sunset, in awe of all the ways nature has of showing off. After about an hour on the beach, I began the drive back to my room, tired from the hot water but jarred awake once I realized I'd be coming 'round the mountain in complete darkness. Street lights were only available for the first and last tenth of a mile. The rest of the drive was pitch black.

My arms were so stiff from clasping the wheel I had a hard time removing them when I finally did get back. I drove a maximum of 10mph the entire time, taking more than 2 hours total and making everyone go around me, but the important thing is that I made it.

That's when I ended up in the bar, looking for anything open in the small town after dark that still served food. Thankfully, the bar's kitchen hadn't closed yet to feed the trivia goers. I found a sandwich on the menu and socialized while I waited. I slept soundly that night, with a full belly and fond memories.

Ignorance is bliss.

I walked out of my room the next morning, ready to send off New Zealand with doughy pancake goodness. I wanted to get moving since I had to be back to Auckland by 5pm, with a flight at 8pm, and I was still at least a 3-hour drive away. The gravel in the makeshift parking lot crushed under my feet as I rolled my bag towards the car, leaving a visible trail along the way.

I walked to the driver's side to unlock the door and that's when I saw it; or should I say "them." The scratches, dents and general evidence of an accident mutilating the side of the rental car. I had been driving on the left side of the road, closest to the mountain, and apparently I got a little too close. I was so petrified I hadn't even noticed. Didn't feel a crunch, didn't hear a noise and didn't see it when I parked to get food the night before. But here it was, and it looked *bad* in the daylight.

I tried not to panic. Everything was fixable. I might have to skip the pancakes but there had to be a solution. I gathered my things in a hurry, forgetting my favorite bathing suit in the process. I'd bought it in Santorini and it was the only swimsuit I owned that made me feel confident. I left it on the drying rack and forgot to pick it back up on the way out. I would realize this later, at the airport. Don't worry, I found a solution for that too. I was in problem solving mode.

I got in the car and called the credit card company. I cited my credit card coverage when I declined the additional insurance at the rental shop. Before I told anyone about any accident, I just wanted to verify it would apply.

"How can I help you?" asked the agent.

"Hi. I want to review the terms and conditions of the rental car insurance policy on my travel credit card."

"Absolutely, I would be happy to help you with that," the agent replied.

After asking some questions to confirm my identity, we got down to business.

"It looks like you're covered up to 50,000 in liability insurance in the event of an accident."

"Great!" I interjected. I made a mental "check" as each of the remaining conditions were listed.

"For coverage to apply, you need to have paid for the reservation in full with the credit card."

Check.

"The cardholder needs to be the only driver on the reservation."

Check.

"And coverage does not apply in Australia or New Zealand."

What? Nooooooooo!

"I'm sorry, can you repeat that last part? There must be some mistake," I asked the agent.

"Australia, New Zealand and Ireland are all countries excluded from coverage," the agent stated matter-of-factly.

"Don't you think that's something important you should tell people?" I was trying to keep my composure, but panic was starting to set in.

When I rented the car, time slowed down as I was made to sign a waiver declaring that if anything happened to the car, I declined coverage and would be personally liable for $4,000 or the price of repairs, the greater of the two.

I vividly remember saying, "No problem, I have $50,000 coverage on my credit card. I'm good!"

Famous last words.

"It's all in the terms and conditions ma'am. We encourage our users to read those. Is there anything else I can help you with?" the agent asked.

It was time to get off the phone. I didn't want the credit card company to get a whiff of my despair.

"No, thank you." I replied. "Have a nice day."

I hung up the phone and got to work. A call agent was the least of my worries. I used my international data to find the nearest hardware store and drove myself there in hopes of finding one of those pens people use to fill in car scratches. You have to start somewhere.

I parked right outside of the hardware store so I could show the car to the attendants if necessary. The first clerk thought I was crazy. Apparently desperate and broke are two traits that do not bode well for customer service interactions. After some searching, we found a pen but not in the color I needed. There was another hardware store 2 hours away, on the drive back to Auckland.

Pancakes were officially off the table. I hit the road, on the hunt for car redemption.

By the time I had to explain my predicament again, I was much more precise. This time the gentleman at the store followed me out to get a look at the car.

"Bollocks!" he exclaimed. "That's not $4.000 worth of damage."

"That's what I'm saying!" I felt relieved to have gotten through to someone.

"I'm sorry, I don't have what you need here but my friend owns a body shop down the street, go see him and tell him I sent you."

I managed to get one person on my side. I just had to repeat the process. Down the street I went, this time pulling into an auto shop that was equipped to handle body work and collision repair. I gave the short version of my story one more time.

"Hello. I'm a tourist. I love New Zealand! Unfortunately, I scratched my car without realizing it last night. If I return it in this condition, I'll be charged $4,000. I'm poor. Help!"

That was the gist of it. I also threw in the store clerk's name for good measure. The owner took pity on me and came to have a closer look.

"This looks like a lot of it can buff out," he said while running his hands against the scratched finish.

He went to get a handheld buffer and came back, getting right to work. I watched as the white rag resembling a round mop mechanically whirred away on the panel, hoping this would work.

When he pulled back from the car, I breathed a sigh of relieved. Most of the obvious scratches came off. There were some that had gone past the paint that needed to be filled in, but the car was returning to its original blue color as opposed to mountain residue white.

The owner went into the garage and came back with 2 jars of paint.

"One of these should be a match," he said as he dipped a brush into the first can. He did a test stroke along the side of the car panel, but it was a little too bright. He wiped off the paint on a rag and dipped his brush into the second can. This time, the match was near identical. Not as much shimmer, but the same base color.

He stepped back to admire his handiwork.

"That's the best I can do without coming in another day or ordering new parts," he said.

"It's amazing!" I replied. I handed him all the New Zealand cash I had left and expressed my sincere gratitude. For the moment my problem had been solved, or at least patched over.

I got on the main highway back to Auckland, feeling much better. There was just one little thing nagging me -- the rim on the front driver's side wheel was still scratched, and anyone who looked at it would be compelled to take a closer look, discovering the hack paint job. It was like a giant arrow threatening to reveal my secret and I had to do something about it.

I went back to my map and stopped at another hardware store on the road back to Auckland, the fourth stop on my auto repair tour of New Zealand. This shop was having problems of its own. The power was out and as I walked up to the sliding double doors, a woman came from inside and manually pried the doors open.

"I'm sorry," she said, "we're not able to attend to customers right now because our power went out."

I launched into my story.

After hearing me out, she suggested I go to a tire place nearby and see about getting a rim replacement. I did just that, but the manager said he couldn't help because he'd have to order a rim that matched the others and it wouldn't make it by my deadline.

I went back to the store with the power outage and implored the woman once again for a solution. That's when she suggested I file the rim. As crazy as it sounds, I was up for anything. She went back in the shop and came back with a giant metal file, like a nail file only industrial-looking. She also brought out some silver paint. My mission, should I choose to accept it, was to file down the raised ridges of the rim and paint over any telltale spots with silver paint.

So sometime around 2 p.m. on my last day in New Zealand, I sat crossed-legged outside my 4th hardware store somewhere in the North Island of New Zealand, filing the rim on a rental car I wanted to return and walk away from debt-free. I didn't do half bad, either. I could have a future in rim filing if I ever needed the gig. Unless you knew to look for it, you couldn't notice the damage.

The store clerk approved. She also noted that the credit card machines were separate from the building lights and still operational as she handed me my receipt.

I learned a valuable lesson that day. Sometimes you wake up expecting pancakes and life gives you a literal wreck instead. You can give up, or you can find an industrial-sized nail file and fight. Always choose to fight.

2.1 Picking the Right Destination

Where should you go for your first solo trip? This is a personal decision and there's no wrong answer. It's exciting to know that you have a world of options. You can start small with a day trip nearby or go big with a round-the-world voyage. To help aid you in your decision making, let's discuss some of the key factors in making your choice.

PROXIMITY

If this is your first solo trip, by all means start small. Visit a neighboring city or state. Take a day trip out into nature. Try a local hike you've never done before. The key is to prove to yourself that you're capable of managing an itinerary, finding your own way and being alone in your own company. The more you do it, the easier it becomes.

When you go far away, you have to deal with friends and family being on different schedules or businesses not accepting credit cards. These obstacles are manageable, but it's best to ease yourself into the world of solo travel if possible. If you go somewhere nearby and it goes off without a hitch, you'll feel emboldened to keep traveling and testing your own limits.

If you live in the United States, budget airlines like Frontier, Allegiant and JetBlue make flying within the continental U.S. easier and more affordable than ever, with periodic sales boasting $30 one-way fares. If you live in Europe, the same goes for RyanAir and Easy Jet. By signing up for the airlines' email lists, you can be among the first to know when these sales pop up. Maybe Nashville, Tennessee wasn't on your radar originally, but for $40 one-way it could be.

LANGUAGE

A language barrier can be an impediment for first-time solo travelers. Aim for destinations that speak English or cater to tourists enough that the staff all speaks English. Sometimes getting lost in translation is fun, but other times its 2 a.m. at a train station in the Czech Republic and you can't find anyone to tell you why no buses or taxis have passed by.

There are many apps that can help you with language limitations, including Google Translate that can translate street signs and menus, but it's best to start off somewhere that you can communicate easily since it reduces your chances of getting lost and missing crucial information, like the fact that buses don't run after midnight in some cities in the Czech Republic. Or that cars are towed after 5 a.m. at a parking lot that turns into a weekend farmer's market in Cannes, France.

Again, ease yourself into this. If you're a first-time solo traveler, you'll find lots of exotic destinations speak

English, including Australia, New Zealand, Belize, Ireland and the Bahamas.

POLITICAL CLIMATE

As a traveler you should feel free to explore the world at your discretion, with caution, but there are certain places that are undeniably safer than others. I went to law school in Baltimore and spent 3 weeks in Bali. Before leaving for my trip, I asked Alexa to compare the crime rates of both. There are an average of 55 murders a year in Baltimore per 100,000 people, compared to .5 a year in Bali. The numbers don't lie – Bali was safer. It felt safer. I could walk around at night and interact with locals without feeling distrustful or watched.

In contrast, my trip to Buenos Aires, Argentina made me nervous. There was a feeling of political unrest and upheaval. Access to cash at ATMs throughout the city was not guaranteed. The people spoke about rebellion and Argentina's troubled history. I was scammed upon arrival by a taxi driver I got at the airport. This is a product of many factors – including the fact that it's a big city – but it's spurred in part by the political instability of the region.

To be clear, you should be vigilant everywhere. You're also free to explore countries that aren't exactly "safe" – I've been to Mexico several times and loved it so take travel advisories with a grain of salt.

That said, countries with steady political climate and very few incidents include Iceland, Canada, Denmark, Singapore, the Netherlands and Norway.

ACTUAL CLIMATE

Is it rainy season where you're going? If so, this could affect the activities available to you. Are you switching hemispheres? The seasons are opposite, so your summers are their winters. Are you looking to go for a certain festival, like to see the cherry blossoms bloom in Japan or experience the midnight sun in Finland in July?

Another consideration is temperature extremes. If you get lightheaded in the sun, you might want to avoid Arizona. If you can't handle extreme cold, an Alaskan cruise isn't for you. Weather can also impact the time you visit a destination. I went to the Czech Republic in the middle of a terrible heat wave and had a miserable experience that tainted my memories of the country since it wasn't properly equipped with A/C or ventilation. Had I gone in the fall I would have had a completely different experience. Weather, and the timing of your visit, are something you must research before booking.

RELIGIOUS BELIEFS

If you don't like being covered up, perhaps visiting a Muslim country isn't for you. If you don't like voodoo or the supernatural, you might want to avoid New Orleans. Religious beliefs aren't a determining factor when it comes to choosing your destination, but it's one you should consider.

In all cases, you should be respectful of customs, attire and holy spaces. It's necessary to cover your shoulders in Asian temples, for example, and considered disrespectful to get a tattoo of Buddha. The best way to learn about other religions is by experiencing them firsthand. While they may not be in tune with your beliefs, there's something peaceful about entering a place of worship.

If you have an open mind, then I recommend visiting somewhere with a completely different religion than yours. You can learn a lot about the driving beliefs of others and discover that we're more alike than different.

Notably, religious observations could affect operating hours of businesses. Some countries have silent days or a week where the nation has a religious observance, like

China for Chinese New Year. Make sure to check if your visit falls on an important holiday or ceremony.

Religious monuments that should be on your bucket list include Angkor Wat in Cambodia, Christ the Redeemer in Brazil and the monasteries of Meteora, Greece.

EASE OF TRAVEL

Whether you're traveling for business or pleasure, going somewhere new should be fun. That is more likely to happen when things fall into place and traveling is easy. There are many questions you should ask in assessing this final factor.

Does your destination have strong WiFi? Are credit cards readily accepted? Is there A/C or heating? Do people drive on the right or left side of the road? What is the currency and is the conversion rate favorable to you? What kind of outlets do they use? Is there good public transport? Uber? Can you find basics like water, a grocery store and a pharmacy?

You can go on a trek through the Amazon, with no WiFi and bugs the size of your face, because you are a badass and you can do anything, but I wouldn't recommend this for someone just starting out.

For American travelers that want an exotic escape with ease of travel, consider Puerto Rico, Ecuador or Belize. There are American power outlets, dollars are readily accepted and people speak English.

2.2 About Travel and Health Insurance

Travel insurance is purchased to protect you in case of a cancellation, health emergency, natural disaster, lost luggage, rental car damage or change in itinerary. With airlines offering basic economy tickets now that do not include any kind of change privileges, this can be a worthy investment so long as you read the fine print.

Not all travel insurance programs are created equal. Some negate benefits for complications associated with pre-existing health conditions. Some require you to have proof of extenuating circumstances to change your itinerary. Some don't cover you if you have competing coverage from a travel website or credit card.

You can purchase travel insurance for one trip at a time or for a length of time to cover multiple trips, like a year-long policy. If cash is due at the time of the transaction you will likely have to pay and be reimbursed after the insurance company determines the expense is covered. Make sure to keep all of your receipts and relevant documents.

You might be wondering, is travel insurance necessary? It's up to you. Typically, an American health insurance policy doesn't work abroad. Rental car insurance is a must since you never know what will happen when driving on unfamiliar roads. I recommend having insurance of some sort. If you have it through your travel credit card and don't need additional insurance, this is a cost/benefit analysis you need to undertake.

Popular travel insurance companies include Allianz, World Nomads and Travel Guard.

2.3 Cash and Credit Cards Abroad

In most parts of the world, cash is king. Aside from the stewardess only accepting credit cards for in-flight purchases or hotel wanting a card for incidentals, you'll be hard pressed to find anyone that turns down this form of currency.

CASH

The best way to get cash is to withdraw some directly from the ATM at the airport when you arrive. You may have to pay a higher ATM fee, but these machines are most likely to be stocked with cash, it's a safe location with plenty of surveillance and there are people around to help if something goes wrong. You'll sometimes need local currency to leave the airport. For those who have it, the Charles Schwab credit card refunds you for ATM fees incurred while traveling, even the inflated airport fees.

I avoid using ATMs too often while traveling since you never know when you'll find a reliable one and using one lets people know you have cash on you, but you shouldn't withdraw the maximum amount of cash every time either. In a 2-week trip, I might visit the ATM three times – once at the airport, once for pre-planned withdrawals and one for unexpected expenses that popped up along the way.

Bring American dollars with you in case of an emergency. At a minimum, have $50USD on hand before you leave. This should be enough to get you from the airport to the hotel if anything comes up. As a general rule, I do not recommend exchanging money before your trip. You'll find a better exchange rate withdrawing from the ATMs at your destination directly and U.S. dollars are widely accepted as back-up cash. I also do not recommend getting traveler's checks. It's an outdated practice.

Whenever possible, avoid currency exchange booths. They charge you high transaction fees and rarely have the most favorable rates. In some countries, like Cuba, you have no choice. The ATMs are not guaranteed to work so you'll need to bring all of your cash in American dollars and exchange it upon arrival. Avoid sketchy exchange places recommended to you by strangers. It may sound like a better rate, but there are many scams out there.

Finally, open a Charles Schwab card to get refunded all ATM fees.

CREDIT CARDS

It may surprise you to learn that credit cards are not accepted everywhere. The most widely accepted credit cards are Visa and Mastercard. Make sure whatever card you take doesn't charge international transaction fees, otherwise you could be paying an extra $1 or more per purchase. When you're paying with a credit card abroad, you will have the option of processing the charge in USD or the foreign currency – always choose the foreign currency because you get a better exchange rate.

If you get a travel credit card, benefits can range from rental car insurance to lounge access and free flights and hotel stays. At a minimum, having one can eliminate international transaction fees and save you money on things like checked luggage.

Always notify your bank and your credit cards before you travel abroad to avoid having your card declined. Also check to see if there are any withdrawal limits while abroad. Only carry as much cash as you need.

STORING MONEY

Don't keep all your cash and cards in one place in case something goes wrong and you lose your wallet or bag. Instead, keep a credit card with a decent available balance stashed somewhere in your luggage for emergency use only. I also like to keep cash in my luggage, usually in nondescript pocket of a clothing item tucked away inconspicuously with everything else.

Another good hiding spot is in a bag of tampons. You can open one up, remove the tampon and stuff cash or paperwork inside the applicator. A thief isn't likely to inspect feminine hygiene products thoroughly.

I personally don't use room safes often since other people can have the key, but you can certainly use one and look for one when choosing a place to stay.

2.4 What to do in an Emergency

It's not a matter of if things will go wrong, but when. Once you change your mindset to realize that you cannot control everything while you travel and that things will happen, you'll start to see emergencies more clearly and be able to react with a clear mind instead of panicking.

I have lost my wallet twice, lost car rental keys, been locked out of an AirBnB, been too late to check in to a hotel, been rained out for a long-planned tour, had activities cancelled on me after I paid to get there, got sick abroad, had an ATM eat my only debit card, got lost abroad, been assaulted abroad and ran out of money abroad. You name it, it's happened to me. The important thing is, none of these situations were the end of the world.

You can't live in fear of what might go wrong. Something inevitably will, no matter how well you plan or how diligently you scope out Google street view. But there is an answer to every problem, and sometimes the solution is better than what you originally had planned. Other times it sucks and costs you a ton of money. That's life. At the end of the day, you can always earn more money. You can always buy new things. The important thing is your health, wellbeing and safety.

HEALTH EMERGENCY

Regarding your health, it's possible you'll get sick abroad. Our bodies have a hard time adjusting to different diets. I recommend bringing your own stash of over the counter medications, like Tylenol and Benadryl.

Sometimes you think you're being safe by sticking to foods you know but in reality, those ingredients aren't as fresh and could also affect your stomach. I had this experience eating pizza in Bali and got the dreaded "Bali belly." Don't be afraid to eat street food, just make sure you're eating from somewhere that looks reasonably hygienic and has a line with other people whose responses you can observe before chowing down.

If you get ill and need medical attention, there are urgent care clinics throughout the world. Many times, you can pay for a visit out of pocket. If you require hospitalization, airlifting or emergency ambulatory services, this is where it comes in handy to have travel insurance.

When I was in Thailand, I met someone who had to get stitches on their finger after feeding an elephant and getting too close to the teeth. The procedure was quick, and he was able to pay for it himself in cash. Don't panic if something happens to you – people get sick all over the world.

Take your time and acclimate to new surroundings. Things like altitude sickness or jetlag can knock you down a for several days and ruin your trip if you ignore them in the very beginning. Make sure you schedule time to rest and always listen to your body. If you have something planned but don't feel up to it, reschedule. Better to miss something than to push yourself too hard and end up in a bad situation.

Note that airlines will not let you fly if you're visibly sick. It's a risk to them since they may have to turn around mid-flight or make an emergency landing if something happens to you. Flying also exacerbates existing conditions like the stomach flu or a sinus infection.

INCIDENT INVOLVING THE AUTHORITIES

If something happens and you need to interact with the authorities, stay calm and be respectful. They won't always speak English. I dealt with authorities in France after my car was towed and frequently while driving in countries like Mexico. I also talked to a ton of policemen in Italy while on the hunt for an extra cute one whose picture was posted in a female travel group on Facebook, but that's neither here nor there.

Always get proof in writing if you need to file a report for any loss or theft. Make sure that you get the names of everyone you speak to and take plenty of pictures. I have friends who had their AirBnB robbed and others that got into a car accident while riding in an Uber. These companies are notorious for shifting blame on third parties and denying refunds or compensation so document everything you can and be diligent about following up on the claims process. This is another instance where travel insurance would come in handy.

If you lose your passport abroad, this is also fixable. Not ideal, but fixable. You'll need to contact the U.S. embassy and speak with the consular section to schedule an appointment to come in and show other documents, like a license and your travel itinerary. The process moves quicker if you have a copy of your lost passport and a police report documenting the loss.

If something more serious happens, like a natural disaster, attack or evacuation, your safest bet is to head to your local embassy. You can find the address on Google or in any regional travel guide. Stay up to date with local news before you visit to a destination, but don't let headlines deter you. There was a volcano exploding for weeks in Hawaii while most parts of the island were carrying on with business as usual.

FLIGHT OR RESERVATION CRISIS

If you lose your luggage, airlines have tracking systems to help you locate lost bags. Most of the time it'll come in on a later flight and the only inconvenience is having to return to the airport. If the bag gets broken or damaged in transit, see if the airline or your travel credit card will reimburse you for the loss.

If you miss a flight or a connection, the good news is that there are other flights. Yours is not the last one to that destination. Even if you have to wait a day, the agents at the check-in counter can reschedule you for another flight. If it's your fault you missed the flight, you'll probably fly standby on the next flight. If it's the airline's fault, they will automatically reschedule you and might even cover your hotel accommodation should you need to stay overnight.

The only time airlines won't accommodate you is if you have the most basic fare. This happened to me on a flight to Portugal. I paid $200 but it was mostly taxes and fees. My actual fare was $29. I missed the flight because I left my passport in Naples (the flight was leaving from Miami,

2 hours away) and the agent was originally going to reschedule me for the next day but when she saw the price of my fare there was nothing she could do. Since I didn't have insurance on that flight, I missed my trip.

If something happens and you need to cancel a flight or hotel reservation that is nonrefundable, don't forfeit that money. A website called SpareFare allows you to sell your prepaid tickets and recover some of the price. It's worth checking out in the event of last-minute changes to your schedule.

The fact is, life can happen at any time, anywhere. You have the ability to solve problems while traveling in the same way you do at home. Don't panic, keep receipts and reports and have an emergency contact that you can reach easily.

SOLO TRAVEL TIP #3
Bet on "Rice and Beans" at the Chicken Drop in Belize

Normally, I'm not a gambler. I'm terrible at card games. I take $20 to a slot machine and watch it slowly deplete to nothing, one lever pull at a time. So the last place I expected to find myself while in Belize was at the weekly chicken drop at Wahoo's, placing bets and crossing my fingers that a chicken would poop on my number.

As a preliminary note, no chickens were harmed in the making of this story. Quite the opposite — those were the most well fed, morally supported chickens I've ever seen. They live a free-range life, aren't eaten on any given day and are even local celebrities. But I digress.

Wahoo's is a bar and lounge located on the beach in San Pedro, Belize. Guests walk from the sand, up weathered wooden steps to the open deck and bar inside. There are three flat screen TVs and a well-stocked liquor selection, but the draw on Thursdays is towards the back of the room.

That's where you can get chicken drop tickets. Rules and conditions are displayed prominently throughout; they take the chicken drop seriously around here. There are five rounds. Tickets for each round are a different color. The first round starts at 7:00 p.m. and there's supposed to be another round every half hour or so, but time is relative in Belize. Not to mention, you have to wait till the chicken(s) decide to go.

I got one ticket for each round, ready to strap in for the long haul. I got two tickets for the mega round with a prize of BZD$1,000. All other rounds had a prize of BZD$100, which came out to USD$50.

I looked at the rainbow-colored assortment of tickets in my hand and felt optimistic as I walked out to the gameboard. On the way, I passed the chicken man, also known as the keeper of the chickens. He was barefoot with long dreadlocks and tanned and tattooed skin. Seeing my hand full of tickets, he wished me luck. I thanked him before making my way to the beach to get a good spot for the first round.

The gameboard was massive, a giant square at least 7ft x 7ft with smaller squares inside that all had numbers on them. There were poles set up around the perimeter with ropes draped in between, serving as a makeshift border to keep the crowds at bay and avoid chicken tampering.

When the DJ was ready, he called the chicken man out with the first chicken.

The chicken's name was Rice and Beans. It was formally introduced to the crowd and everyone was encouraged to cheer him on by name. Chickens need emotional support, too. I had my phone on Instagram live, recording the whole thing. Rice and Beans was presented to a random member of the audience and that person placed him on the board to do his "duty."

The chicken man sprinkled corn and feed liberally across the board. The chicken did its thing and went around eating it, happily. We all watched and waited for the inevitable – the winning sh*t to drop.

After about two minutes of edge-of-our-seats anticipation, it happened. Number 57.

I got my camera ready to zoom in on the person who won and their reaction before I even thought to glance at my own hand. No one immediately jumped to claim their prize so I looked down at my tickets briefly.

"Wait -- number 57?" I asked out loud. "I have number 57! In the yellow tickets? Are we on yellow? It's yellow for the first round, right?"

I threw out one question after the next to the people immediately surrounding me. They didn't seem pleased with my lack of comprehension, but I needed to be sure before I got excited.

Someone confirmed that, yes, we're on the yellow tickets and yes, number 57 was just called. I was the winner! The crowds parted as I stepped over the rope border onto the board. I walked towards square number 57, now in need of clean up.

One of the rules and conditions is that you have to bring the poop with you to redeem your money. I smiled proudly as the chicken man handed me a white napkin and bent down to pick up the collateral I needed to redeem for my cash.

I've had big dogs before. A chicken's "drop" was nothing compared to a German Shepard's. I walked to the shop at the back of the bar. The man verified that I had the winning number and we took a picture together before he handed me my cash.

I know it's only $50 (damn exchange rate) but I felt rich. Like I said, I don't gamble. I don't get money just handed to me, no strings attached, so I'd never felt the high associated with it. I see how it could be addictive.

I wanted to exchange my winnings into dollar bills and fan myself with them, after buying a drink or two, but I needed to be smart about it. Unfortunately, I had a long way back to my hotel. The chicken drop was a hassle for me to attend, but I wanted to go so badly that I resolved to worry about getting back later, when the time came.

It was not lost on me that it had been publicly announced to a group of rowdy people that I now had cash. Me -- in my airy dress, looking happy, flushed and very unintimidating. While part of me wanted to celebrate this momentous win, I couldn't allow myself to fully let go because I had to watch out for myself.

When someone asked to dance with me, I noticed all eyes shift to see what my reaction would be. Those watching were wondering whether I was the kind of girl who got down to reggae music. For the record, I am, but I politely declined. Despite wanting to get a double rum and coke and cheers to Rice and Beans, I stuck with a single and took it at a slow pace. I went back to the game and had fun cheering on the other chickens, and after about the third round I decided to call it a night.

Today, I can say the chicken drop was one of my most memorable experiences in Belize because I pulled it off safely. Despite being alone and having to embark on a 20-mile golf cart ride on pitch black, pothole-ridden roads, I have good memories of the evening. It could have gone wrong in so many ways. That's why I stayed vigilant and didn't let the exuberance of winning get the better of me. That's why I made sure to project the image of, "I'm not here to lose control; I'm here to win the chicken drop."

Attending the chicken drop was a gamble, but I did it in a way that I could revel in the experience and protect myself at the same time. As a solo female traveler, that's the sweet spot you should be looking for.

3.1 How to Travel Safely as a Woman

When a woman gets attacked abroad, the media attention to the attack can make other women too fearful to travel alone, and understandably so.

We try to distinguish ourselves from the victim. We think to ourselves, "I would never dress like that" or "I know better than to drink alone." The truth is, the only thing necessary for a crime to occur — and please hear me on this because no attire, level of inebriation or other circumstance ever warrants an attack against an individual — is the presence of a criminal.

It doesn't matter where in the world you live or are visiting. Criminals exist everywhere. I've lived alone for almost 14 years, in major cities like Baltimore and Miami. I travel the world by myself, and it's not always incident-free.

Despite this, I will continue to live my life. I will take public transportation and shared ride services, dine alone, attend activities during the day and night and talk to people I don't know. I hope that you commit to doing the same.

People who travel alone are not uniquely brave or strong – they just push through the fear knowing they'll be rewarded in the end. To help you do the same and have a little peace of mind, let's discuss some of my top safety tips for solo female travelers.

1) Have an emergency contact

I mentioned this in the section on what to do in case of an emergency, but it's crucial that someone knows where you are at all times. You can share your phone's location or send a pre-penned itinerary to your friends and family members, but make sure someone expects to hear from you every day. Exceptions apply, obviously if you're somewhere without any service, but almost everywhere has

WiFi nowadays. Check in with someone back home and don't go completely off the grid.

2) Be wise about money

Never flaunt your money. Get a crossbody bag or one of the discreet travel wallets you can wear under your clothes so someone can't just pull a purse off your shoulder and run with it. If you win cash, tuck it away. Avoid using large bills. Don't carry more cash than you need. If credit cards get stolen, you can get that money refunded. Once cash is gone, it's gone. Some people go as far as to get a decoy wallet that they can turn over if they need to.

Don't keep all your money in one place. Have cash and cards tucked away in different places so if you lose a bag or something gets stolen, you can keep going.

3) Don't look lost

One of the most valuable pieces of advice given to me as a lifelong city dweller is to walk with purpose. You can't meander around a street. Don't look lost. Don't be distracted on your phone, making a call, sending a text or listening to music on headphones. You need to know where you're going and walk there determinately. You need to be able to hear if someone is coming up behind you. Don't make yourself easy prey.

Do your research before you go somewhere. Don't leave a restaurant or store without knowing what direction you're walking in or better yet, have transportation secured. This holds doubly true at night.

4) Check your accommodations

Sites like Booking.com and TripAdvisor allow you to filter reviews, so you can look for key terms like "safety" and "solo" to see what guests before you have thought. Make sure you're in a safe neighborhood. Double check that parking won't be an issue. Aim to be on a higher floor to avoid ground floor break-ins or easy visibility. Ask to be near the elevator so you don't have to roll your luggage past every room in the hall and alert the entire floor to your presence. Use your peephole (if you have one) before opening the door and use every lock available to you when you're in your hotel room. Carry a spare doorstop to wedge under the door, just as an extra means of protection.

5) Keep your passport with you

I've gone back and forth on this, but you will sometimes need your passport for different activities, transportation, etc. and a photocopy won't cut it. Not to mention, you never really know what's safe in your room. I suggest keeping your passport on your person while traveling. This is where a decoy wallet, hidden travel wallet or secret clothing pocket comes in handy. If someone tries to forcibly take your passport and you're in danger, remember that anything lost can be replaced and the most important thing is your safety.

6) Scream "fire!"

This is an oldie, but a goodie. My mom used to instruct me on this when I walked home from school alone. People are naturally curious. Believe it or not, people run towards fires. They want to see what's going on for themselves. Not as many people run towards "murderer," "rapist" or the general catch-all, "help." If you need assistance and want to call a crowd quickly, scream, "fire!" Add this to your list of words to learn in the primary language for your destination.

7) Leave your valuables at home

Diamond rings, family heirlooms, your Dooney & Burke purse – these things are all better left at home. That way you can guarantee you'll return to them and they'll be in the same condition as when you left them. Traveling doesn't carry that same guarantee. Take the risk if you don't believe me, but don't test out this theory with your most prized possessions.

Not to mention, you want to avoid attracting unwanted attention to yourself. You'll already have people watching you just by virtue of being a female. You may not realize it, but they are. You want to blend in and not look like a rich American prime for robbing.

8) Stick to public places

You're an independent woman and you're free to wander about dark alleys at night, but I wouldn't recommend it, especially if you're new to the surroundings. Instead, stick to public places. There's safety in numbers. If possible, always have someone escort you to your transport at night. Public places also tend to have authorities available. Even remote locations like national parks will have rangers.

9) Get a whistle

While pepper spray and stun guns are frowned upon by TSA, you have alternatives. In this case, a whistle is your friend. It's small and light, so you can fit it in your bag without a fuss, and it goes through security without issue. What's more, one loud blow and you'll scare the life out of whoever is attacking you. The last thing they want is attention.

10) Avoid alcohol

I love a good rum and coke. I love margaritas. I love piña coladas, both in and out of the rain. When I'm traveling, however, I avoid drinking too much. I'm going to drink because I'm on vacation, but I'm not there to get wasted/hammered/sloshed/trashed/drunk/housed/plaste red. I just want to have a delicious cocktail, see pretty things and return unscathed. As enticing as it is to indulge further, solo female travelers look like even more of a target when inebriated.

If your main goal is to drink, stay home and go HAM on a few bottles of wine with Paris movies playing in the background. A few bottles later and it'll be like you're right there.

11) Do planned activities at night

Nighttime can be tricky. You don't want to go to a club or bar by yourself but at the same time you don't want to just stay at the hotel. The solution? Go on a guided tour or other nighttime activity. I've taken an evening bar crawl tour in Athens, attended a late-night flamenco show with dinner in Spain and gone midnight kayaking during the full moon in Miami.

You don't have to be resigned to your room after sunset just because you're a female that's traveling alone. Plan an activity so you're not aimlessly wandering unknown streets and are on a safe, controlled outing instead.

12) Know popular scams

There are so many scams out there that it's hard to keep up. I don't recommend trying to learn them all – doing so will burn you out and make you lose faith in humanity. Instead, research your destination before you go to learn what the scam of the moment is. Check in on Facebook groups or traveler threads. Is it pickpocketing? Something to do with hotel keys? Old ladies handing out suspicious, coma-inducing apples? Whatever the case, best to be aware so you can avoid them and be extra careful under those circumstances.

13) Learn basic self defense

I'm not talking Jackie Chan's style of self defense. I'm talking about how you can inflict the most damage with minimum effort. What are the soft spots (eyes, nose, throat, groin) that you can aim for? How can you best leverage your weight and size to buy you time to get out of a dangerous situation and make your escape?

The last thing I want you to do is engage your attacker in combat. I want you to be able to maneuver out of things like being chocked or someone holding your wrists. Those are the moves that matter most in keeping you alive, more so than the TKO dropkick. Though if you have that and someone comes at you, finish him.

14) Keep your technology hidden

You don't want to go around flaunting your latest laptop, camera or GoPro. Leave these things at the hotel, and make sure they're tucked away and not in plain sight. Don't leave them in the backseat of a car or anywhere that's visible.

What may seem like a "cheap iPhone" to you is worth a lot of money elsewhere and can be all the incentive people need to break in, steal or vandalize your property.

15) Get a fake love life

This suggestion is a little out there, but if you find yourself constantly getting asked why you're alone and how it's possible you don't have a boyfriend, a fake wedding ring might help. Nothing ostentatious, but enough to support your story that your fiancé, Bob, just couldn't make it on this trip because of prior work obligations but wanted you to have a good time in his absence, because he's the best. Thanks, Bob!

16) Learn the local language

I've touched on this already but knowing a few basic key terms will not only help ingratiate you to locals, it can come in handy in case of an emergency. Water, restroom, help, telephone, fire, please, thank you – these are all essential terms you should know or have handy on a cheat sheet nearby.

17) Don't let your phone die

Screen addiction aside, cell phones are our connections to everything nowadays. It's how people track you if anything happens to you. It's how you can call for help or pull up a map. We all know phone batteries die notoriously fast.

Have at least two backup batteries and your charger with you at all times so you can take advantage of wall plugs whenever you see them and charge up any gadget that's low on juice, backup batteries included.

18) Know local emergency numbers

There are different emergency numbers everywhere. In China it's 119 and in England it's 999. Know the emergency phone number for wherever you're going and with any luck, you won't have to use it.

19) Deflect unwanted attention

I love to smile, but I've learned that I need to be picky with who I deal smiles to while traveling. I can't walk around like the chimney sweeper from Mary Poppins, tipping my hat and greeting everyone I meet with an ear-to-ear grin. It brings unwanted attention, and some people take it the wrong way.

Fight the urge to be friendly and smile less. Don't acknowledge people who are soliciting you, even if you just want to be kind and say no thanks – they'll take it as a go-ahead to try and change your mind.

Keep a stiff upper lip, shoulders back and head up. Walk straight past any unwanted attention and don't acknowledge or feed into a situation that you don't want to progress any further.

3.2 Choosing the Right Accommodations

You have several options when it comes to where to stay, such as a hotel, AirBnB or other privately-owned rental properties, house sitting, hostel, campground or couchsurfing. These are listed by my order of preference.

HOTEL

If you're looking for a hotel, start by searching on the right search engine. For Southeast Asia travel, I like to look on Agoda. For U.S. travel, I look on Expedia since I get a member discount and price check on TripAdvisor since they aggregate search results from other companies.

I choose a hotel based on the customer experience versus the star rating. I could care less if it's 5 stars with a spa and 24-hour gym. I care more that the last 50 people who've stayed there have had a 5-star experience, even if they didn't have so much as an in-room coffee pot. The best way to narrow down your search is to filter by price and then rank by user rating, high to low.

Now that you've narrowed down your options, it's time to start reading reviews. As I mentioned previously, certain websites let you filter through reviews by keywords. I search for non-negotiables like "WiFi" to see if people have commented on the connection and "hairdryer" to see if one comes in the room.

Don't disregard small hotels. They can be just as comfortable as their lavish counterparts. Just note that small hotels don't always have a 24-hour staff and you need to let them know if you're checking in late. Read the terms and conditions for the exact time they close.

I had this happen to me in Santorini when I arrived after midnight to find the front office closed. I wandered around for half an hour asking nearby businesses for help, before finally stumbling across a white sheet of paper taped to a white wall saying "Ruiz, your room is X." Thankfully the door was open. I was preparing myself to sleep on the beach.

AIRBNB OR OTHER PRIVATELY-OWNED RENTALS

AirBnB has become controversial in the tourism space lately since the demand for short-term housing has inflated the prices of rents in cities like Lisbon and New York City. Owners realize they can make more money charging per night and decide to stop renting it out monthly/yearly residents. This is a problem with all short-term rentals, not just AirBnB, but AirBnB is the most well-known company in the space. Two popular alternatives are VRBO and HomeAway.

If you decide to use AirBnB (I have on several occasions) I recommend that you rent from a Superhost. The title is hard to get and even harder to maintain. It requires that homeowners get near perfect reviews, and they'll go above and beyond to maintain the designation. I would never book a property that didn't have reviews. It's also important to check the terms and conditions. Some properties charge you for late check-in or cleaning.

If you're traveling for a month or more, you might be able to find a better price on a rental if you book through local sites. Google "Craigslist equivalent in X country" to find the best forum to browse. When I was living in Australia, I found a furnished studio through Gumtree for two months.

HOUSE SITTING

Some people are professional house sitters, traveling full-time with free accommodations. I only recommend this strategy if you're willing to put in the time it takes to build your profile. The best rental opportunities go to people with experience and glowing reviews. You can't just decide you want to be a house sitter and secure a week in the South of France the next day.

House sitting is also an investment, with several websites requiring you to pay a monthly fee to be shown on their listings to potential clients. This can be a great way to see the world safely since you get an entire property to yourself but is not for someone who just wants to dabble in the practice. Websites like TrustedHousesitters or Mind My

House are good places to start if you're interested in pursuing this further.

HOSTELS

I am not a fan of hostels. Personally, I take deep comfort in knowing that there's a deadbolt between me and any other humans at night. This could be one of the reasons I'm still single. I'm also a light sleeper. The thought of having to listen to the noises that a dozen other people make at night sounds like torture to me. I have gotten private rooms at hostels before, but only with *en suite* bathrooms. The last time I shared a bathroom I ended up showering in a stall, like a horse.

You may enjoy staying at a hostel. The prices can be insanely low, like $4 a night, and they are great if you want to meet other young, rowdy people. I am an old lady. I like to go to bed in quiet surroundings after having taken a shower in an enclosed space just for me. Call me crazy, but I don't want to have to call bottom or top bunk.

I have heard horror stories about women waking up with men on top of them in shared dormitories so if you go this route, make sure you lock your belongings, sleep with tights on at night and avoid co-ed sleeping arrangements.

While it's typically a younger crowd that uses hostels, you get people of all ages from all over the world. As I mentioned, some have amenities to make them worth a visit even if you're not a guest for the night – case in point, the world-famous Broken Shaker Bar at the Freehand Hostel in North Miami Beach.

Hostel life can be fun and affordable, just know that it might not be the most comfortable or restful. Whether you should stay at one depends on your priorities and traveling style. You can find vacancies for hostels on standard booking sites like Expedia (the room type will say "dormitory" and prices will usually be far below average for the night), or you can search specialty sites like Hostelworld.com.

CAMPGROUND

I've camped outside and frankly, it's not all that fun (refer to my Grand Canyon story at the beginning of this book). If you're camping solo, it means you're carrying all your things. It means there's no one to watch your site while you walk to get water or use the restroom. It means you're sleeping on the ground.

As we've established, I'm a fan of comfort. I'm sure glamping could be fun, and it has been trending in recent years, but old-fashioned camping is not for me. That said, it might be for you. Cheryl Strayed camped on her hike up the Pacific Crest Trail.

When I was in Antiparos, Greece there was a campground that sold out in summer with families and students alike. If the weather is nice, consider websites like Gamping, Hipcamp and Tentrr that offer everything from campground permits to pre-built luxury tents on public and private property.

Lock your tent at night by using a travel lock to bind the zipper handles from the inside. Have proper lighting for when you're walking at night. Make sure you know where you're going. Try to camp in a populated area as opposed to isolating yourself in the wilderness. Have something on you to defend yourself – you never know when an animal might come by and having a small knife is better than nothing.

COUCHSURFING

Couchsurfing is a broad term to define you staying in someone's home, presumably on their couch. You could couchsurf with a friend that now lives abroad. I've stayed with people I met before and was grateful for their hospitality. You could also choose to couchsurf with strangers. There's an app by the same name that allows you find potential matches. I've heard it's easier to find a placement as a solo female traveler than a solo male traveler, which concerns me. Also staying on a couch brings us back to that lack of a deadbolt situation. You're open and vulnerable to whoever comes in the room.

I am too anxious to be a couchsurfer. I wouldn't be able to sleep because I'd be convinced every little noise is my new housemate coming to kill me in my sleep. Dramatic, I know, but these are the things that run through my mind when I'm in a foreign country at 3 a.m.

I will note that a friend recently returned from a trip to Japan where she utilized couchsurfing to stay with an older man, his wife and his mother. They let her have a room in their house. The man used to be a frequent traveler but had to stop to take care of his mother, so now having couchsurfing guests is a way to bring the world to him. They looked after my friend, made sure to pick her up from the train station every night and shared stories and fond memories over family dinners, to which she was invited. Her story encouraged me to remain open about this option and refer it to others.

I had a similar experience at a homestay, a family's house where they open up rooms to tourists. The family was so welcoming and made my trip that much more authentic and meaningful. I found the homestay through a well-known hotel booking site. I've also experienced something similar when staying at BnBs, though they're slightly more hands off. Staying with a family can greatly enhance your travels, and you're not limited to the Couchsurfing app or study abroad programs when looking for them.

Another option is to look for groups that match female travelers who are in the same area. The Girls Love Travel (GLT) group on Facebook has been working on a home sharing/couchsurfing exchange. This is one way to make the pool of strangers you're picking from less intimidating and already somewhat vetted. At the end of this book, I've included a list of helpful groups, apps and websites to help you meet other solo travelers, including the GLT group.

3.3 Mastering Transportation Abroad

Navigating your way around a new place can be intimidating. Whether it's your first time riding in the back of a tuk-tuk or you're trying to decipher subway maps written in Dutch, it's both a challenge and a thrill to figure out how to get around while you're on vacation. Here are some tips to make the whole process a lot smoother.

PUBLIC TRANSPORTATION

First and foremost, I encourage you to take public transportation. By its very name, this is a method of transport intended for general use. It's not meant to be complicated. It's not meant to give you a headache. Even if you can't pronounce the name of a stop, you can read well enough to know that you've just arrived at it.

Depending on where you're visiting, public transportation may actually be the quickest way to get around. Before you leave, make sure you have the name of the closest station to your hotel written down, and that you know what time the trains and buses stop running. I once found myself in Rome at 1 a.m. after the train closed (didn't read my Europe for Dummies closely enough there) and had to figure out alternate transportation late at night.

TAXIS

You other option is to take a taxi. I personally can't stand taxis and I can't wait for the rideshare economy to run them out of business. I find it ridiculous that you can rack up the meter even when you're sitting in traffic not moving anywhere. I hate their pushy sales tactics and they can be aggressive.

That said, most of the world has not wised up to this yet, and taxis are quite common outside the U.S. In some places, Uber and Lyft are banned and taxis are your only choice. If that's the case, always make sure the meter is on so at least you know what you're being charged and the driver can't just make up a price. Don't put your bag in the trunk; take it with you in the backseat so the driver can't hold it hostage.

Write out your hotel address in the native language. Someone at the front desk can do this for you. This way you can show any random taxi driver that you hail an address they'll understand. When you're paying, count out your money to the driver. I was the victim of a scam where my driver insisted I gave him a smaller bill than I did and gave me change for the smaller bill.

Ask your hotel to order the cab for you, that way you're guaranteed someone will show up and aren't waiting by the side of the street unnecessarily. They also tend to use reliable companies.

DRIVING ABROAD

As you saw from my New Zealand fiasco, driving abroad can be challenging. Make sure that you have an international driver's license if you need it. You won't always need it – check the terms and conditions of your rental agreement before you go and save yourself the $20 and in-person visit to AAA if you don't.

Make sure you have car insurance in one form or another. As mentioned in the insurance section, sometimes having conflicting insurance policies can negate your coverage, so stick to one policy.

Certain rental venues are pushier than others and can charge questionable fees. Instead of being loyal to one brand, i.e. "I'm only ever going to rent with Alamo," I suggest you check the rating for that particular franchise location before renting a car. You can do this by searching for the location on Google, such as "Alamo rental car Las Vegas." Read the reviews to see what the basis of any complaints are – long lines you can handle, a $500 deposit might be tougher to swallow.

Scamming culture can vary depending on your location, not the brand, so don't be deterred by smaller name shops. The most important thing is the experience other customers have had with recent rentals.

Try to plan long drives during morning hours or before sunset to avoid falling asleep on the road. When I did a road trip throughout Arizona, I'd finish hiking by 5 a.m. and be at the hotel by 7 p.m., to avoid driving long monotonous roads after a long day.

Have some sort of GPS. If you're using your phone, have either a SIM card with data or an international data plan.

You can also have a mobile hotspot. Otherwise, rent a GPS device that you can attach to your dashboard. The locally programmed ones are more likely to have remote roads and accurate directions than Google or Apple Maps anyways.

If you're driving on the other side of the road for the first time, stick to open spaces while you practice. Note that many roads across the world will barely be wide enough to fit one car forcing you to pull into a clearing to let another vehicle pass. Don't let this rattle you.

It's likely that any tolls will be charged straight to the vehicle and billed to your credit card after the fact. If not, it could be worth investing in a fast pass or prepaid toll device. Your agent will tell you about this when you go to pick up the vehicle.

Similar to the hotel, if you're arriving late make sure the car rental counter is 24 hours. It's possible you'll have to take a shuttle or get checked in with another company. If so, you'll see a sign at the company's counter at the airport.

SHARED RIDE SERVICES

Shared ride services are competitively priced, timely and convenient. You know exactly where your driver is and how much your ride is going to cost you. Friends can track your location through these services to make sure you're OK.

The downside is that they're not always available in your location, rates can skyrocket during peak times and in countries where they're contested the drivers can be shady, asking you to sit up front or act like it's a friendly pick-up.

Always make sure you sit in the backseat no matter what your driver says. As a solo female traveler, it gives you crucial space and time to react if your driver tries anything. If they don't let you, cancel the service and wait for another ride.

<u>HITCHIKING</u>

I would not recommend hitchhiking as a solo female traveler. I know, between this and my feelings on hostels you might think I'm the most uptight traveler in the world. What's more, I know females that have hitchhiked successfully. They're adventurous souls. My mantra is that if there's even a .001% chance that this endeavor is going to end up with me as a lamp, I'll pass. I'm fairly certain the odds while hitchhiking are much higher than that. You may luck out, but you might not, and it's for the latter reason that I can't in good conscious advise you to go this route, no matter how many self-defense classes you've taken or whistles you own.

3.4 Making Friends and Beating Loneliness

A lot of people avoid travel for fear of being lonely. The good news is, it can be conquered. First, if you plan your trip well enough, you won't have time to be lonely. From sunrise to sunset you'll have activities to go to and be so tired that you knock out afterwards, before doing it all again the next day.

The best place to start making friends is to join a tour. I love day tours and short experiences because they give me the opportunity to try something new without committing me for too long. Conversation naturally strikes up at these events. Work on your personal elevator pitch – 15-20 seconds on who you are, where you're from and what you're doing there. You'll be asked this a lot.

When you're dining alone, don't look at it as a social endeavor. Look at it as a chance to feast on delicious foreign food and also take advantage of the free WiFi in the restaurant. If you've been touring all day, you've probably not had the time to post on Instagram or respond to messages on Facebook.

Do these things while you're waiting for your food to arrive. That way you're being productive, frugal and learning how to enjoy your own company. I usually have breakfast on the go, grabbing an egg sandwich from a corner café.

If you want to put the phone away during dinner, bring a book with you instead. Sitting at a bar is good for getting seated faster and they almost always serve a full menu in addition to drinks. If you do this though, you'll be sending out a more social message than if you just get a table for yourself. I've done both.

See if you can meet up with friends in the area or connect with like-minded people through online groups. There are Facebook groups for female travelers where you can reach out to see who else is in the area at the same time that you are. There are also official apps and websites meant to link travelers, like Tourlina and Wandermates. I have included a master list at the end of this book.

When you're traveling, it's easy to miss modern comforts. From air conditioning to public bathrooms that you don't have to pay (or squat!) to use, there's no place like home. Adapting to a different lifestyle can make loneliness worse. Your support system feels miles away as you deal with dropped calls and conflicting schedules.

Don't get discouraged by temporary pangs of loneliness. I'm a seasoned solo traveler and I get them when I see a couple kissing at a famous spot, or a family taking a picture together at one of the mandatory photo stops on the way into an attraction. Those are hard to pose for alone.

It's normal to be lonely, but if you put yourself out there it will be near impossible not to meet people along the way. You can plan a meeting through groups or apps, go to places where you'll find people with shared interests like a yoga studio or art exhibit, or just be open minded about the small interactions you have along the day. You could end up befriending the front desk clerk at your hotel or tour guide on a day trip.

Don't let the fear of being lonely stop you from buying that plane ticket. It gets easier with every trip, and soon solo travel might even be your preferred method of travel as you discover your own best travel partner – yourself.

SOLO TRAVEL TIP #4
Checked Bags and Cobblestones Don't Mix in Cinque Terre, Italy

I love Italy. It's one country I keep coming back to. I've been to the main cities, including Rome, Florence and Milan, but the place I always dreamt of visiting was Cinque Terre. Their colorful houses perched on the waterside cliffs looked like heaven, and I fantasized about strolling the Italian Riviera in a sundress while eating gelato.

The reality turned out to be somewhat different, except the gelato. I had plenty of that.

I arrived in Monterosso in the middle of July, during one of Europe's record heat waves. I'd packed poorly, with a huge checked bag. I was going to be in Europe for several weeks and foolishly thought I'd need that much clothing to be prepared. My bag was brand new, bought just for the trip, but had to be tossed when I got home from the damage it sustained.

The first challenge I faced was getting off the train platform. The elevators were broken, so I had no choice but to go down the stairs. I cringed as the bag hit every cement step on the way down. I got out to the curb only to realize there were no taxi drivers in Cinque Terre. Not at the train station, anyway. There were a handful of people with a vehicle for hire in the area, but only if you had the hookup.

Having no other choice, my bag and I tackled the cobblestone streets, guided by the GPS on my iPhone toward the hotel's general direction since it couldn't locate the exact address. I walked down a long path, under a tunnel, through a market and up several small streets before finally arriving at what looked to be the right place.

I was sweating profusely. Wrapping my hair up in a bun wasn't doing anything, I kept waiting for the breeze to come and graze my neck, but it never did. When I reached the final steps to get to the entrance, I sobbed a little.

I'm convinced Italian people eat so much pizza and stay so skinny because their life is one never-ending StairMaster. It's rare to find elevators in Italy – I'm surprised the train station had them. The architecture is ancient, and they won't risk damaging the integrity of a building to install a modern amenity such as an elevator when there are perfectly good stairs available. I braced myself for the final effort, dreaming of A/C and a cold shower at the end of this last stretch.

To be fair, the suffering was my own doing. Had I not packed so much, I would have had a much easier time getting around on foot, but I'd shackled myself with nearly 75 pounds of luggage. It was like carrying around an extra person.

This realization weighed on me as I struggled to lift the luggage up the stairs. They say positive affirmations are good for you, so I cheered myself on.

"It's going to be alright, Jen."

"That which does not kill ya, am I right?"

And my personal favorite, "there are worse places to be than lugging your bag up a flight of stairs in Cinque Terre."

Eventually, I made it to my room and was able to rest up. The heat was unbearable. Something about the humidity combined with unrelenting sunlight and heavy physical exertion made me want to crawl into bed and never leave.

Eventually I did wander out. I ate gelato back to back at different shops. Because I *could*. I took pictures by the harbor. I rode the train to other areas (Cinque Terre is made up of five towns). I had such a good time that I almost forgot the ordeal that was waiting for me when it was time to leave.

Thankfully, I made friends with the hotel owner and she called a taxi for me when it was time to go a few days later. This time around, I only had to get my bag down the stairs and through a small side street. I was eagerly anticipating my exclusive Cinque Terre taxi ride.

I dragged my beaten luggage to the main street where I was told to wait and stood by the side of the road. When I saw a taxi approaching, I stood up. Red haired man driving a taxi – he fit the description.

I stepped towards the middle of the road, waving at the driver to get his attention. He didn't look at me, though, and just kept driving.

Alright, no problem. I'm not very good at hailing a taxi. Maybe he just didn't see me. I was wearing tights, a t-shirt and sneakers after all (my usual travel attire) so I wasn't exactly breaking necks. I would wait and try again on his way back down. This was a small town and there were only so many ways he could navigate. He'd have to pass by me again at some point to get to the train station.

On his way back, I tried harder to get his attention. You would think he'd acknowledge the girl flailing her hands overhead by the side of the road, maybe saying something like, "I'll be right back." After all, he was driving 10mph with the windows down.

The third time was the charm. The next time I saw him, he stopped and I got in before he could object. The ride was less than a mile to the train station, but I felt like I'd dodged a bullet. Roller bags and cobblestones just don't mix.

He left me at the entrance to the station and, as predicted, I struggled to lift my mammoth bag up the cement stairs to the platform. I was sitting next to the bag, three out of four wheels barely hanging on, when I saw an older Italian couple get off a train on the platform across from me. They made their way to the elevator. I was tempted call out and tell them it was broken, but they were on the other side of the tracks and I didn't want to be that screaming, hobo-bag-having American.

Instead, I watched as they walked into the broken elevator and held the ground floor button the whole way down, a trick I hadn't been aware when I'd simply pushed the button several times without success.

Yes, I love Italy. But sometimes I wonder if Italy loves me back.

4.1. How to plan the perfect itinerary

If you only have a short time at your destination, planning is essential. You don't want to spend an hour in the morning researching where to go and how to get there when you only have 48 hours in a new city.

Also, like I mentioned, traveling can serve as a safety blanket when you're alone, making sure you have plans, know where you're going and are expected to be places at certain times.

If planning is not for you and you're a "go with the flow" kind of gal, go on ahead and skip to the next section where we talk about clothes. Otherwise, hang in there with me cause I'm going to take you through my 5-step process for planning a trip.

Step 1: Brainstorm ideas

This is the fun part. Once you know where you're going, you can do general research to see what kind of sites the destination has to offer. You can search related hashtags on Instagram, go on Pinterest for inspiration or even ask friends who've been there before for advice. Make sure you hunt down the unusual and little-known sites. Atlas Obscura and travel blogs in general are great for this.

Compile a master everything that sounds interesting to you. This is your brainstorming list.

Step 2: Prioritize

Now it's time to start weeding down some of the activities. Is anything seasonal and closed during your visit? Are some things too far away? Is there anything you know you just have to see, perhaps of the unicorn onesie variety? Start crossing things off your list and moving them around in order of priority.

Step 3: Get a blank calendar

Now it's time to get a blank calendar and start filling in the time slots. Put in your flight information. Account for how much time it'll take you to pick up your checked bag and get to the hotel from the airport. Give yourself a half hour to an hour to get settled. Right there you've already spent 3 hours of your first day without going anywhere.

It's important to have a calendar so you can visualize putting all these pieces together. It'll also give you a good overall idea of how packed your schedule is, not to mention writing helps you better commit things to memory. If you add contact information like phone numbers and addresses, it could serve as your master itinerary for the trip.

Step 4: Fit events in like puzzle pieces

If anything has a pre-determined time, like a show at 7:30 p.m., make sure you add that to your calendar before moving forward. Now, do you absolutely have to go to the Louvre when you're in Paris? Is this your top activity? Research the best time and day of the week to go and put that into your calendar first. This might be a weekday in the morning, for instance.

Factor in the time it will take you to get there and give yourself 1-4 hours depending on the museum. You could spend days in the Louvre. It's just an example we're using here but if you go, you'll want an audio guide or tour to help you navigate the highlights and not waste time being lost.

After that, fit in your second highest priority onto the schedule. Ideally for a 3-day trip you should be able to knock out a handful of things you want to see at the ideal times. After that, fit in the remaining pieces. Work based off proximity. If you're already at the Louvre and a restaurant on your list is a block away, stop there for lunch. If you can't see everything, that's more reason to return.

Step 5: Schedule down time

Always schedule down time. I give myself an hour or more at my accommodations before dinner to unwind after the day and take my time getting dressed. I also like to allocate "free time" after an activity in a desirable location so I can take advantage of an adjacent shopping district or scenic route and just wander.

Just because you have a plan doesn't mean you can't go for a leisurely stroll and give the universe a chance to surprise you.

4.2 What Should You Wear?

One of my favorite hobbies is collecting dresses from around the world. I love the vibrant fabrics and unique designs I find everywhere from Southeast Asia to Central America. Usually, the products are hand stitched and sold at a steal price.

Dresses are my primary clothing item when I'm traveling. They're easy, look great in pictures, pack and fold easily and are respectful. Many of my dresses extend to the floor, perfect for a temple visit. It can be hard to know what to wear when you're traveling. Let's go over some of the main occasions you'll have to dress for.

AT THE AIRPORT

I applaud anyone who can go on a long-haul flight with uncomfortable clothing and shoes. Sure, you might meet someone at any time, and some people just like to look nice, but when you're about to board a 6+ hour flight comfort and ease come first.

To go through security, you should always have socks on in case you need to take your shoes off. It's not great to walk barefoot on those mats. Wear sneakers for shoes that are easy to take on and off. You'll also need to do a significant amount of walking in an airport. Consider it your exercise.

Wearing a bra with an underwire might get you flagged for further screening by the full body scanner, as will having a scrunchie on your wrist or wearing anything with excessive buttons or zippers. I like to wear tights and a t-shirt so there's minimum risk of getting stopped. Also, it's nice to have tights while on the airplane so that the bottom of your pants don't touch the bathroom floor. You won't want to wear shorts or anything less than tights because it gets really cold at 30,000 feet and at a minimum, you'll want your legs wrapped.

Layers are great for flying. I always have a hoodie in addition to my t-shirt and bring my own blanket. You should have a small bag of toiletries on your carry-on in case you need to freshen up, like brushing your teeth or putting on face moisturizer since it's really dry on an airplane.

Make sure to have a change of clothes in your carry-on as well. It's good to prepare for the worst but hope for the best as far as luggage goes, so if anything happens to your checked bag it's good to know you have clothes to change into until it arrives.

IN CONSERVATIVE COUNTRIES

Some countries are more conservative than others. How you dress will depend on where you're heading. In Brazil, you can walk around wearing pasties and no one would look at you twice. In Morocco, if you show some leg, you're going to get unwanted attention.

You will need to cover your hair to enter a mosque, your shoulders to enter a Buddhist temple and don a sarong wrap to enter certain monasteries. Outside of sacred spaces, however, each country will differ on the level of dress code enforcement. In Iran, for instance, women have to cover their heads with a headscarf, wear a long skirt or loose pants and a long-sleeved tunic or short that reached the knee. In Dubai there are no requirements, but Westerners are encouraged to dress modestly.

Not all Muslim countries are created equal, so you could be fined for your clothes or punished like a local under Sharia Law. The stricter places to note and be weary of include Saudi Arabia, Sudan and Burkina Faso.

If you need to cover up from head to toe in hot weather, opt for loose fabrics to allow for ventilation and the occasional breeze. In places where you need to take off your shoes to enter a home or temple, wear sandals or flip-flops instead of shoes with laces.

It can be frustrating to tone down your attire for the location you're in (anyone else getting a high school flashback?) but you will be more comfortable when you blend in and aren't experiencing unnecessary hassle because of your clothing. It's also important to be respectful of other cultures, so as much as you want to wear a crop top, understand it is just not normal and accepted everywhere.

IN WINTER

I dislike going to winter destinations because it throws packing light out the window. You can fill up your carry-on bag with outerwear alone, which is why I wear as much of mine on the plane as possible. If you don't pack well, you'll freeze and have a terrible time. So first and foremost, accept that going somewhere during the winter is going to require you to check a bag.

If you're going somewhere wet or icy, like glacier hiking or skiing, you should wear snow pants. Essentially, they're pants that will make you look like the Michelin Man and keep you from looking cute in any of your pictures, but they'll keep you warm and most importantly, dry.

My secret winter clothing item is a pair of alpaca socks. I cannot rave about them enough. I bought three pairs in Peru, intending to give them as gifts for my dad, and kept all three. You won't need to double up on socks. You won't need long underwear. One pair of alpaca socks (genuine alpaca, not some knockoff blend) will not only keep your feet warm, your toes will be sweating while everyone else gets frostbite.

IN EXTREME HEAT

My biggest concern in extreme heat is my hair, if only because I'm prone to severe frizzing and the transformation between Panteen Pro-V hair and frizzy hair makes people do a double take and go "ugh!" when they see me. If this sounds like you, pack a headband or scarf or bandana – anything to help your hair look cute in hot, sweaty times.

Otherwise, warm weather destinations are a dream for light packers. Bring a few sundresses, a bathing suit, cover up and flats and you're all set. Choose light colored fabrics since black stores heat, and wear light fabrics like cotton or linen. If you're desperate, they sell little portable fans that you can wear around your neck, like the people at Disney.

Avoid colors that show sweat easily, like gray. Don't forget to wear sunblock. Bonus points if it's also in your makeup and lotion. Regarding accessories, carrying an umbrella when it's not raining may seem strange, but it's an effective way of escaping the sun. You may have seen Asian tourists doing this to avoid tanning/burning.

Make sure to stay hydrated and drink plenty of water. Cold food items, like ice cream, will bring down your body temperature, so take advantage of the excuse to grub. I also recommend that you go sightseeing in the early morning and evenings and take a nap midday, when the sun is at its hottest.

FOR AN ADVENTURE

Ready to go on an adventure? The most important thing you'll need are good shoes. You want shoes with a rubber sole and good traction. I also have a hiking jacket that I like to bring along with me when trekking. It's by Marmot and the material is warm but also somewhat water repellant so if I get caught in the rain I won't get soaked.

If you're going out on the water, it's a good idea to bring water shoes. You never know what you'll step on in the ocean or rivers. I also bring a microfiber quick dry towel with me and a change of underwear since it's not great for your feminine composition to be in a wet bathing suit bottom all day.

Always avoid wearing jewelry on adventures, even the cheap kind, as you'll likely lose or damage it. I bring a workout outfit with me everywhere I go, not because I'll be using the gym at the hotel (ha!), but in case I need to be outdoors. Pack at least two workout outfits and several pairs of socks.

4.3 Taking Insta-Worthy Shots on your Own

One of the questions I get asked most is how I take my photos when I travel alone. It's not easy! You can hire someone to take photos of you. I did this with Flytographer and while it was a great experience, it's not at a price point where it can be done often. If you're lucky, you might find photographer friends while traveling, especially if you're running in a digital nomad community

Another option is to hand your phone/camera off to a stranger and hope that they 1) don't get their thumb in the picture; 2) get you at a good angle; 3) get you in the shot, period; 4) make sure there's good lighting; 5) don't run off with your camera forcing you to engage in a foot chase in a foreign country. That's a whole lot of wishing and hoping.

I will sometimes hand my phone to a stranger, depending on the circumstances. I look for people traveling in groups (harder for them to run off if they're with others). I also look for female Millennials since that demographic is most familiar with Instagram, flattering angles and the importance of taking 10-20 shots to find one viable photo. They use the burst feature generously.

The last photo capture method, and my preferred option, is to get a tripod and host your own mini photoshoot. You can get a professional camera (DSLR) for $200 on eBay. Research the brand you like and features you want. Stores like Best Buy allow you to test out the latest models so you can see for yourself. Make sure it's a good weight and portable since you'll need to be carrying it everywhere you go. I have a Canon and so far, it's served me well.

You'll also want to make sure you have the right lens. They have wide angle shots allowing you to capture more scenery or zoom lenses for when you'll need to get up close. Lenses are actually more important than the body of the camera itself and quite costly. Do your research before purchasing these as well.

At the end of the day, you don't need a fancy camera to take good pictures. I still have an iPhone 7 and it works great, although the storage is finally getting full, with more than 20,000 images. You just need something to capture photos of you, preferably with a timer, otherwise you'll need to invest in a remote.

Next, get a tripod. I got mine for $20 on Amazon. It's portable and does the job. I can also fix different attachments to it, so it holds both my phone and DSLR. I also have a selfie stick, although I have to admit that I hated myself when I gave in and purchased one. If you will be out in nature a lot, or just want a more versatile tripod, consider getting a GorillaPod. The legs bend and mold to the way you set them so you can easily attach it to a tree or fence.

I used to have a GoPro and people love that you can get wide shots on there, not to mention underwater footage for that fun trend everyone is doing where you see the meniscus line in the ocean or pool, but I didn't use it much so decided to get rid of it. Often times when I'm on underwater activities they'll offer pictures as part of the deal and not having the GoPro allows me to better immerse myself in the experience.

Once you have your basic equipment (we're talking bare bones here – something to capture images and a tripod to hold said device in place of a human) you'll want to find a scenic spot that's not crowded. There's nothing worse than trying to stage your own photo shoot in the middle of a tourist hot spot. People will walk in your shot, your equipment could get knocked over, and frankly it's awkward to pose when everyone is looking at you. Those are the times when it's best to take your chances with a stranger.

If you have the time, find a secluded place (in the daytime) and get a picture of the iconic scene you're hoping to capture form a hidden spot. This way, you can take your time and alter your poses if necessary when you see how they're coming out.

After, you can edit your pictures using different apps or software I use professional editing software called Lightroom. It's a part of Adobe Creative Cloud and requires a monthly subscription. If you ever see influencer selling their Lightroom presets, those are basically photo filters for Lightroom. Instagram also has an option for you to alter the photo settings manually, from brightness to saturation, that will do in a pinch. I also sometimes make use of my phone's auto enhance feature, depending on how it looks.

Taking good photos on your own is easier than you think. With the right equipment, a little bit of confidence and some editing, you'll be taking professional quality images in no time.

4.4 Tips for Packing Light

I know the feeling. You want to take everything. You worry that when you get there, you'll be missing the crucial piece or accessory that your outfit needs to be complete. It's especially frustrating because you already own it and can pinpoint its exact location in your closet.

The important thing to remember is to not take packing too seriously. Learn from my Cinque Terre mistakes. If you forget something, you can always get a replacement or make do as is. Maybe you won't have the perfect outfit on, but I guarantee you will be the only one who notices.

Packing light can be beneficial to you in many ways. It can save time because you don't have to stop by baggage claim after a flight, or before a connecting flight. It can save money as airline tickets include less and less nowadays. The cost of a checked bag could be up to $100 each way! Bringing a carry-on only also allows you flexibility to take advantage of comps that are offered in an oversold situation. That $500 travel voucher isn't as sweet if you have to deal with the pain of locating your bag after. Finally, if you're taking advantage of hidden city ticketing and not intending to take your full flight, you'll need to be carry-on only (though I don't recommend this).

While becoming less common, most American airline carriers allow you to bring one carry-on and a personal item and set limitations on size versus weight. This is the ideal situation because you could have a roller bag and duffel bag and fit two weeks of clothing and essentials with ease. Avoid overstuffing the outer pockets on the luggage since doing so (and expanding the zipper to full capacity) could trigger the gate agent to ask you to put the bag in the dreaded metal frame to see if your bag fits.

If you're traveling on a European airline, your carry-on is regulated by weight so even if you are allowed two pieces, you might be limited to bringing on 20 pounds between the two of them. Airline policies vary but the most common weight restrictions are 15 lbs (6.8 kg), 18 lbs (8 kg), or 22 lbs (10 kg). This severely limits your packing, and in some instances, you'll need to check a bag. I would still aim to bring a carry-on sized roller bag and check it instead of bringing it on board, since anything larger is a hassle to transport on your own.

Roll your clothes instead of folding them; it saves space and allows you to pack them tightly. I also use space saver bags to compress clothing further, especially when I'm traveling with bulky items like snow pants. If you like to have clothes sorted and don't want to dig around your bag to find an outfit, consider packing cubes to keep everything separate and organized upon arrival – you can move them straight from your luggage to the dresser at your hotel when you arrive.

In general, the earlier you board the plane the better shot you'll have at securing coveted overhead bin space. You don't need to have your luggage directly above you on the plane but aim to not have it behind you or you'll have to wait even longer to de-plane. Note that in some countries, your board from the front and back of the plane after taking a shuttle to the runway, so it's a mad rush for storage space. When all else fails, you can use duty free bags to give you some extra room that doesn't count against your carry-on allowance.

SOLO TRAVEL TIP #5
If You Have a Bank Account, Address and an Ex in Another Country, You Lived There

When I was in law school I lived in Sydney, Australia for 6 weeks. I say "lived" because at the time, that's what it felt like. I had an Australian bank account, rented a studio in Paddington and took the bus to work every morning.

I was interning for an Australian organization that analyzed and made recommendations to the government about areas in need of legal reform. I let years of advanced education pass me by without taking advantage of the opportunity to study abroad, so I enrolled in a class on international law (a prerequisite to the internship program) and applied to program around the world in an effort to squeeze a trip into my $100k+ in tuition costs.

I received two invitations — Canada and Australia.

Knowing what I know now as a seasoned traveler, I wouldn't be so quick to disregard Canada, home to wonders like ice caves and the Aurora Borealis. At the time, however, Canada seemed dull. I grew up in Philadelphia, so it was easier to get to Canada than it was to get to get to Florida.

I picked Australia without hesitation. I didn't realize I'd be going by myself. I didn't realize it'd be winter there even though it was our summer. I didn't realize Australia was an in-demand travel destination. I just knew I had an invitation, and a chance to do something different. Only a handful of my classmates elected to complete an internship abroad, and I was the only one person heading to Oz.

I was definitely not in Kansas anymore.

For six weeks, I lived close to the city center. My job was in a large skyscraper downtown and every day I got to experience corporate life – take the elevator up 30 floors, settle into in an office with floor to ceiling views of a major metropolitan city and do important work.

Despite the grandeur of it all, I was nostalgic for my old life. I was in Australia at a time when the conversion rate wasn't favorable, so I was eating a lot of rice with soy sauce for dinner to stay within my means. I wasn't getting the Australian humor on TV and couldn't stream any of the shows I liked from home. My mom, who I talked to daily, was asleep when I was awake.

These feelings were especially pronounced during what I call the 3-week hump. That's the point after which it stops to feel like a vacation and starts to feel like real life.

It wasn't until I met a guy that my feelings about Australia started to change. Typical, I know, but this particular guy was 6'2", handsome, with blonde hair, blue eyes and a physique carved from years of lacrosse. Normally he would have been out of my league, but they don't have sugar in Australia like they do in the U.S. and my snacking was limited thanks to my budget constraints, so I was at my skinniest. For our purposes, let's call him Mr. Perfect.

It's a miracle he stuck around too, considering I projectile vomited on him after our third date. It was an accident – we'd gone out for a seafood dinner and I had bad mussels.

At least, that's what I think happened. It might have been the wine – for some reason wine can have an adverse effect on me, but he was a connoisseur and I wanted to play along with my new sophisticated role. Whatever the case, something didn't sit right.

We were in his apartment watching a movie after dinner when I started to feel nauseous. I attempted to make a graceful exit, telling him I was tired and needed to call it a night.

"Do you want me to drive you home?" he offered, pausing the TV and looking concerned.

"No, don't be silly," I replied hastily. "I can just get a cab outside."

After some insistence, he let me leave unaccompanied. Of course, Mr. Perfect lived in the penthouse, so I had to hold my nausea in on the elevator ride, all 14 floors down. I barely made it to the outside of the building when I was brought to my knees, vomiting my expensive dinner all over the asphalt.

I was struggling to catch my breath when I heard movement behind me. I froze.

"You're clearly not feeling well. Please come back upstairs and let me help you."

I was mortified. I wanted the vomit-stained asphalt to open up and swallow me whole right there. I couldn't turn to look him in the eye, and at the same time I was so sick that running away didn't seem physically possible.

I didn't have many options, so I agreed to follow him back to his apartment. The only problem was that to get there, we had to take the elevator again. This time, 14 floors up.

I suffered through every inch of the ascent. It was like my stomach was being forcefully shoved into my throat. I thought I'd left all I had on the pavement, but I feared I could be wrong.

Somewhere around the 8th floor, I knew I was definitely wrong. There was going to be a round two, and I prayed that we made it out of the elevator on time.

I don't know what was wrong with me. I had never been so violently sick before, and to date I've never had another incident like it. The timing could not have been worse, with the real victim in this situation being Mr. Perfect.

By some miracle, I made it off the elevator without hurling my life away. It took every ounce of willpower I had in me to hold it down. He went to open the door to his apartment and as he turned the deadbolt to let me in, I couldn't hold it in any longer.

Like the scenes that you see in crass movie parodies, my insides erupted and hit him square in the middle of his back with such force that he was pushed forward. The vile, neon orange substance spilled not just all over him, but on his lush white carpets.

Being Mr. Perfect, he reassured me that everything was fine and made sure I was taken care of, despite the whiplash he'd suffered at the door. He lent me his room for the night (a brave move considering his sheets were also white) while he slept on the couch. I was so sick that I was certain at any point I would stop breathing and die. What's more, after the embarrassment I just suffered, I wasn't sure that would be a bad thing.

The next morning, I snuck a peek into the living room and saw Mr. Perfect on the couch, shirtless. I may have drooled a little – in my condition it was hard to tell. Either way, I blew it for sure. That's OK, cute guys who can take you vomiting on them in stride and live in penthouses come along every day, right?

To my surprise, he actually wanted to see my again. We ended up dating for the rest of the time I was there. I rode on the back of his motorcycle to the Sydney Harbour and we took a day trip out the Blue Mountains. When my internship ended, I wanted to stay. But alas, I had to finish law school and go back to my apartment – you know, real life.

We drifted apart over time and distance (being a world apart can put a strain on a relationship), but I will always remember the summer I lived in Australia. It may have been short, but it really happened, and somewhere out there is a neon orange stain on a carpet to prove it.

5.1 How to Fit Travel into Your Busy Schedule

It's hard to find the time to travel when you have real world responsibilities. I put off traveling for nearly a decade despite having every opportunity to do so, and on the school's dime to boot. I was worried that if I left, I would lose my standing in student government races or not be able to participate in Model U.N. competitions. Those same eventually morphed into, "I can't travel because I'm up for a promotion" or "I can't travel because I have cases to handle."

The point being, there will always be a reason not to go. Life will keep throwing things your way and you're going to have to keep knocking them out of the park, like the badass multitasker you are. You can't let surviving life stop you from living it. Sure, we all have bills to pay and important things to do, but if you don't start prioritizing travel in the same way, all you'll ever do is work.

Start by taking short trips somewhere. If you have off on weekends of certain days of the week, take a day trip in your immediate area. You'll be tempted to sit at home and relax, which is what we all like to do when we get time off but force yourself to make the trip. Once you get there, you'll wonder why you didn't visit sooner.

Not a fan of short trips? Roll over your vacation time and take longer but less frequent vacations. One long trip a year with several weekend trips in between allows you to see more than you think.

Make a friend at work that can cover for your while you're away. Bring back gifts and souvenirs for the office when you return so they'll begrudge your travels a little less. If you travel for work, try to extend your stay. Bookend a conference with two days at your destination so you can actually take in the sights.

Remote work is becoming more and more popular. See if your job will allow you to try working from home or somewhere abroad. You can also start a location independent business or offer your services in the gig economy, allowing you to take on assignments as you see fit.

Life gets busy. If you don't find the time to travel even when you're swamped, you may never find the time at all.

5.2 Taking an Adult Gap Year

All work and no play leads to one burned out, do-it-all lady. If you don't take my advice and overexert yourself, you might reach the point where you're in need of an adult gap year.

What is an adult gap year, you ask? It's like a sabbatical, where you take a break from your job to refocus on your career path and life in general, usually while traveling.

Unlike a sabbatical, you're not guaranteed to have a job when you get back, so you want to consider this move carefully. However, if you've been stuck in a rut or just need to shake up your daily reality, there are ways to pull it off. You could start working remotely, sustaining yourself with work you can do from anywhere. You can also go somewhere with the intent of volunteering or working abroad. Venues will host you in exchange for labor, from farming to teaching, and there are even paid volunteer positions with government or NGO programs.

People do variations of this. I know travel bloggers who've quit their jobs and sold their belongings to travel for 5 years, and I know another couple that's turning a school bus into a motorhome to travel the country in it. Consider that if you're traveling for a year or more you won't need to pay rent, so it frees up a significant chunk of your income. If you have a mortgage, rent your home out for the time you're gone.

This is not an easy transition to make, but the benefits are many and have been explored in novels like "Eat, Pray, Love." I would recommend making a strong push to pay off any debt before doing this and finding ways to generate income while you travel, which we'll talk more about in the digital nomad section below.

5.3 Overcoming Homesickness

There's no place like home, and at no time that you will you repeat this more than when you're somewhere far away with things going wrong. Maybe you can't find food you like. Maybe you can't sleep through the night and have difficulty adjusting to the change in schedule. Maybe you run out of something you need and can't find it anywhere. That's when homesickness starts to hit you.

Because the fact is, things would be easier if you were home. It would be easier to have your local stores with all the things you buy and foods you eat. It would be great to understand all the signs and drive on the right side of the road and be able to have a conversation without a translating device in between.

But traveling isn't always comfortable. It's not always nice and easy and smooth, and that's part of the journey. You may not realize it in the moment, but when you get home you'll laugh at the mishaps, the same way I now laugh at the memory of the jerking motion Mr. Perfect made when struck square in the back.

There are a couple things you can do to cure homesickness. First and foremost, if you need a day, take one. There's nothing like sitting in a hotel bed for a day binging television to make you feel relaxed and at home, even if you have to read subtitles. Sometimes we get so excited to see it all that we overexert ourselves and make traveling less enjoyable.

Next, schedule a time to talk with a family member or friend back home. When I was in Australia, I would schedule an hour-long conversation with my mom on weekends. At the time I used a calling card, because apparently I'm old, but today I use Google Hangouts which is free if you're connected to WiFi.

Find things that remind you of home. One travel study recently revealed that people look for the strange in the familiar and the familiar in the strange. That means if you're at home, you might be compelled to try the new pop-up restaurant featuring something exotic like Mongolian food. If you're traveling, however, you will get excited about every hot dog stand and Planet Hollywood you see, because it's a familiar and known element in an unfamiliar setting. Surround yourself with things that make you feel at home and temporarily calm the sentiment of being displaced.

It could help to keep yourself busy buying souvenirs for loved ones. You'll explore your destination with purpose while conjuring fond memories of people close to you. It could also help to create a daily routine. One of the things we like about being home is the predictability – a set time to wake up, a set drink at the coffee shop in the morning, a time of the week that we go to the grocery store. Mimic your habits in your new surrounding as much as possible to trick your brain into sensing a pattern and feeling a sense of normalcy.

5.4 So You Want to be a Digital Nomad?

A digital nomad is someone who makes a living complete online, typically while traveling (hence the "nomad" part). Unlike participants in an adult gap year, digital nomads have one office: their laptop. You can find them in co-working spaces or in a café or restaurant asking for the WiFi code. Typically, they live at a destination for a few months before moving on to the next; as long as the applicable visa will allow.

Southeast Asia is a hub for digital nomads because of the low cost of living. Countries like Indonesia, Vietnam, Thailand and the Philippines are seeing an increase in this transient, brunch-loving bunch. South America is also a popular place to "backpack" through, since the countries are easily accessible and nightly accommodations are cheap.

Digital nomads make money in a variety of ways. From sponsored posts on social media to selling their own products through an or e-commerce store, the internet is big business. It is possible to replace your full-time income by working online. Note, however, that you still need to work. Many accounts paint a glamorous picture of quitting their 9-5 jobs to travel the world, but the reality is there's no quitting; it's just swapping one job for another.

When you work online, you are responsible for your next paycheck. Whether you're offering services as part of the gig economy or selling digital products, courses and programs, your success comes down to your ability to hustle. It's far easier to work for someone else. If you can work remotely while making a steady income through companies like Amazon or Discover, even better.

Ultimately, most digital nomads choose a home base. It's hard to live without a set address since humans are creatures of habit. If nomadic life is calling your name though, feed your wanderlust and travel as much as you can for as long as you can. After all, the beautiful thing about traveling solo is you have no one to answer to but yourself.

BONUSES

Bonus #1: 16 Useful Apps, Groups & Websites to Meet People Abroad

1. Girls Love Travel

This is the largest female travel group on Facebook. They only allow females as members (and females that have shared accounts with significant others) and there are many subsets of the book, including a Girls Love Travel book club.

This is a good place to ask the audience if you have a question about an upcoming trip or particular destination. They also have a home sharing platform set up through Overnight. Members of the community self-identify through the hashtags #GLT and #GLTLove.

2. Women Who Travel

Women Who Travel is another popular Facebook group, run by Conde Nast Traveler. It's not as heavily policed as Girls Love Travel, which has a weekly dedicated share thread and doesn't allow self-promotion. Here, you can post freely without your submission needing to be approved first. The group is affiliated with a travel podcast by the same name and regularly hosts group trips around the world for women only.

3. Girls vs. Globe

This is a smaller Facebook group so it's more personal. You can connect with the members on here by asking questions or extending an invitation. Just indicate where you'll be and when and see if anyone in the community is available to join you. They also have three subgroups, including a couchsurfing group where you can find opportunities to stay with female group members around the world.

4. Girls Gone Global

If you know Nas Daily you probably know Dear Alyne, since the founders behind both platforms are married. This is the Facebook group formed for followers of Alyne Tamir. They host meetups through an app called Vibely, founded by a group member. There are also themes for the days you post, like "Wellness Wednesday" and "Open Topic Sunday."

5. Wanderful

This is a diverse community for female travelers. They host an annual Women in Travel Summit and have an online collective with workshops, mentoring and robust opportunities bulletin. They also have a home-sharing network so you can stay with other members while traveling. Follow the Facebook page, join the Wanderful Women Who Travel group or sign up for the collective.

6. Tourlina

Tourlina is an empowering female network that you can access via app. They also have a strong social presence across social media. You become a "tourlista" when you join. You can meet other female travelers in the area or arrange meetups with locals – the app is live in over 160 countries and is women only.

7. Couchsurfing

While most well-known for its homestay uses, the popular app also has a function allowing you to search and attend traveler events in your destination.

8. Meetup

I love this website because of the variety of interests found here. There are meetups for everything, from baking groups to soccer fans. I attended a Spanish-speaker meetup in Australia with great success.

You can see the RSVP list ahead of time to know if it'll be a popular event. There are groups that have expat meetups specifically aimed at helping to ease your homesickness; I attended a Fourth of July party in Sydney where people were encouraged to dress up like American icons.

9. GirlCrew

This is a platform for women to make new friends. Whether you're looking for someone to go to the farmer's market with you or travel the world. They offer a premium membership that includes special events and access to private Facebook and WhatsApp groups. The program is based in Europe and offers the most options in that area at the moment.

10. Shapr

Shapr aims to connect people on a professional level. It's like LinkedIn, but more social and with the aim of connecting people in real life. This is a great tool if you're a frequent business traveler.

11. Flip the Trip

This is an app that lets you connect with local travelers nearby. You can ask questions, solicit travel buddies, find a roommate and more. There's also a forum where you can post general questions to travelers already in the area.

12. DownToMeet

If you go to the "discover" section of this website, you'll find groups ranging in title from "Bangalore Gamers" to "Central California Women's Hiking Group." The site is growing as more people join the platform, but it's worth checking to see what's going on near you.

13. Eventbrite

You've probably already used this website at some point to book tickets or RSVP for an event, but did you know you can also browse the site for events happening near you? Start here if you're traveling and want to find an event specific to your interests, similar to Meetup.com.

14. Get Your Guide

This is a private or small group tour website that partners you with local guides on curated experiences, like taking a photo tour or cooking class or day trip somewhere. It's expensive, but the guides are knowledgeable and speak fluent English, the transport is comfortable and they take credit cards. This is a good option if you're in Asia or somewhere you wouldn't be able to easily navigate on your own.

15. Tours by Locals

This site has a similar concept to Get Your Guide – they are the third party that pairs you with local tour guides to host your experience. I used this site for a private tour of Angkor Wat and my experience was incredible – luxurious from start to finish with great photos to boot.

An added benefit of taking a private tour through companies like this is that the driver often volunteers to take pictures and knows all the most scenic spots.

16. AirBnB Experiences

The site commonly known for home rentals has ventured out in recent years into the activity space, offering experiences with locals like making pasta in Italy or meeting a sloth in Costa Rica. You can find everything from photo shoots to architecture tours.

Again, since you're booking through a third party the prices are a little more than if you booked directly with the tour provider, but they take credit card and provide an avenue to state your grievances should anything go wrong.

Bonus #2: 12 Things to Do the Night Before Your Trip

1. Charge your devices

Make sure that your computers, phones, cameras and backup batteries are all fully charged before leaving. This will save you time once you get there and help you enjoy them for longer on your journey. Aim to have more than one backup battery with you, and don't forget to bring the cords to attach it to your phone.

2. Backup your data

The night before you leave is a good time to leave the Google Photos app open for a bit just to back up the photos you already have on your phone. This will allow you to delete that content later if you need the space, and rest assured that it's been saved even if something happens to your phone. You can do this with any work you have on a computer and can use different storage methods like a portable drive.

3. Download movies and books for the road

There's nothing worse than being stuck for hours in economy seating, unable to sleep and with nothing to do. I speak from experience on this. Come prepared with books on your phone – you don't need to bring a separate e-reader and bulk up your bag. Use the Kindle or Overdrive apps. You can also download magazines this way.

Download any Netflix series you want to watch while you have WiFi – a new season of Orange is the New Black can make a transatlantic flight breeze by. Download both movies and series to your phone to access and watch even when in airplane mode.

4. Run through your itinerary

Get everything written out on paper at least once so you can see your itinerary and forward it to any necessary parties. This is a good time to make sure you have addresses and phone numbers of relevant places, like your hotel or anyone who's picking you up at the airport.

Make sure to have your accommodation address in the native language of your destination so you can easily show it to a driver upon arrival.

5. Make sure you have cash

Take out $50-$100 to have as backup cash. You'd be surprised how widely the U.S. dollar is accepted. If for any reason you can't withdraw cash in the native currency when you get there, this should be enough to get you to your hotel and hold you over till you figure something out.

6. Download or print maps

If you're going to be using your phone, download maps to any relevant apps so you can access them without WiFi. You can also print a map if that makes you feel better, just to have a backup.

7. Check the weather

You need to know what you're packing for. Check the weather before you leave and prepare for the highs and lows. Take a small, portable umbrella if the forecast calls for rain.

8. Secure travel documents

Do you have your passport? Visa? License? Boarding pass or train tickets? Important reservation numbers? Now is the time to double check.

9. Call your bank and credit card companies

Make sure you let your bank and credit card companies know that you'll be traveling. Some allow you to do this by submitting a notification online. Some require that you call in. Others don't need any notification at all. Check each of your accounts to see what type of notification, if any, you have to give.

Bring a card with no international fees, and at least one card that's Mastercard or Visa since they're the most widely accepted.

10. Pay your bills

Tie up loose ends at home so you can travel with peace of mind, and not worry about overspending on your budget. Pay any bills that will be due while you're traveling before you go. Return library books that you have out. If you're going to be gone for a while, halt your mail.

You can pay bills while you're abroad, but some companies restrict access to your account depending on location. In that case, you'll need a VPN to log in remotely through your laptop or attempt to make payments over the phone.

11. Throw out perishable food

You don't want to come home to a fridge full of rotten food. Throw out any perishable foods, like milk or leftovers, before you go on your trip. Take out the trash too, so it doesn't just sit there while you're gone.

12. Get a good night's sleep

I know, you're excited. You're going on an adventure! You have a million things running through your head, you're tempted to fall into an Instagram hole scoping out your location or just can't sleep worrying you'll miss your flight.

Try to have a routine the night before you travel – hot tea, a warm bath, maybe yoga or another relaxing workout, sleep=inducing scents like lavender and rosemary. These things can help you get some semblance of sleep before you're up with jetlag or a full schedule on your trip.

About the Author

Jen Ruiz is a solo female travel blogger and lawyer who has been featured by The Washington Post and ABC News for her budget travel secrets. She is also a freelance travel writer with bylines in Matador Network, Paste Magazine, Elite Daily and the Huffington Post, among others.

In 2017, Jen set out to take 12 trips in 12 months while employed full-time as an attorney for a nonprofit organization. She surpassed her goal, completing 20 trips in 12 months to destinations like Greece, Iceland, Cuba, Thailand, Puerto Rico, Italy, France and Cambodia. She went on the majority of these trips alone and doesn't believe in waiting for the perfect circumstances to start seeing the world.

Jen documents her adventures and shares travel advice on her website, www.jenonajetplane.com. She is currently working on her next book with more solo travel stories from her year of adventure. She is active on Facebook,

Twitter, Instagram and Pinterest, feel free to reach out and follow along.

Did you enjoy this book? Your review could make a big difference.

Word-of-mouth is essential for any author to be successful. If you enjoyed this book, please leave a review online. Even if it's brief, it could make a big difference and encourage someone else to dive right in.

Till next time, safe travels!